Entertainer's
Handbook
How to be a Success in the Entertainment Industry

Mike Stilwell

First Edition - November, 2013

ISBN: 1493637231

ISBN 13: 9781493637232

Library of Congress Control Number: 2013920572
CreateSpace Independent Publishing Platform
North Charleston, South Carolina

Copies of this book may be obtained by contacting Amazon.com Request ENTERTAINERS HANDBOOK by MIKE STILWELL

Consultation services are available from the author related to topics covered in the book.

For information: mikestilwellentertainment@gmail.com

Disclaimer

The information in this book is based on my experience as an entertainer. Names, addresses, telephone numbers, and e-mail addresses have been obtained from a variety of sources. To the best of my knowledge this information is accurate. However, some discrepancies may exist and I would appreciate any comments about them. Feel free to contact the author and corrections will be made as soon as possible.

Thank you,
Mike Stilwell

The Author

Mike Stilwell

Mike Stilwell arrived September 19, 1953 in Annapolis, Maryland. His mother will tell you that he was a born entertainer. During his first day at school, while some children were scared, crying or having various embarrassing accidents, Mike pulled his chair close to the teacher and started laughing and telling everyone about the fun that they would have. He has continued to have fun as an entertainer.

His need to entertain was not always appreciated and he spent some time during those early years sitting in the principal's office. However, he did get a break when he performed in the school's play, "The Trouble with Tricks."

He didn't have the opportunity to attend a school of arts during his teen age years. Sports were emphasized at his school but he was more interested in being a class clown. A few years earlier he discovered the thrill of performing magic and soon was a young entrepreneur, sometimes earning a little money but mostly learning to be an entertainer.

After high school, he joined the Navy. It was like magic when he was told that he had orders to a squadron, HLS-35, code name: "The Magicians". He spent his spare time practicing his art and entertaining others during every possible opportunity.

After serving in the Navy for 7 plus years he returned to his beloved San Diego where, during the last 35 years he has established himself as one of the busiest and most favored professional entertainers.

Mike Stilwell also known as "Magic Mike" is recognized for his professional talent, humor, good values and sincere personality. Although he may be best known for his smooth as silk voice and his comedy-magic up close, he has broad experiences in the entertainment field, including developing and marketing magic equipment, owning and operating an entertainment related restaurant, serving as an entertainment producer for a local agency, and teaching magic to a variety of students including some with disabilities. He has the respect of other entertainers and is known to be a team player.

Other entertainers appreciate his expertise and he has always been willing to share the knowledge that he has gained the hard way over the last 35 years. One of his greatest strengths lies in the vast variety of experiences such as having long term gigs (one restaurant for 15 years, another for 8 years). Half of his work is from repeat customers. He has performed at a multitude of locations such as restaurants, streets, malls, ships, hospitals, fairs, homes and trade shows. He has entertained at over 700 Bat/Bar Mitzvahs and hundreds of birthday parties, weddings and graduation parties.

It is not unusual for Mike to have over 200 paid gigs and at least 20 free charity performances a year.

Mike Stilwell has received recognition for his years of work with newspapers, magazines, billboards, and TV interviews. He has received thank you letters from all over the world.

He received a trophy "Magician of the Year" from The Fellowship of Honorable Magicians in 2005. He is a member of The Society of American Magicians, The International Brotherhood of Magicians, Hollywood's famous Magic Castle, and The Academy of Magical Arts. He was the first costumed character to be a member of The Magic Castle. For several years he did close-up magic in full costume including gloves and limited vision as Bumper the Baffling Bunny. He wants to credit much of his success as Bumper to Donna Stilwell (Mrs. Bumper Bunny) for the physical and emotional support she gave during this time.

Mike and Donna Stilwell are the proud parents of two sons: Scott Michael and James Mark and grand-son, Travis Michael Stilwell.

Acknowledgements

First, I would like to thank my mother. Edna Mae Brown LeBow Stilwell I would never have written this book without her. She would not take no for an answer when she asked me to write. She would call me every few months for the last three years to be certain that I was writing and to check my progress. She would remind me of what I knew about entertaining and make me promise to keep writing until this book was completed.

I thank all the other members of my family especially my brothers: Robert, Russell, and James Stilwell and my sisters: Elizabeth Stilwell Morelli and Linda Stilwell Larson for their encouragement and support through the years. They accepted me as an entertainer and did not try to change me.

I thank my sons, Scott and Jimmy and their Mom, Donna (Mrs. Bumper) Stilwell for their patience and support through the years.

The finished product would never been completed without the review and advice of friends especially the outstanding help of John Misteli, who helped to organize, format and edit my manuscript for printing. Thank you, John.

I Also wish to thank photographer Michael E. Johnson

I thank all of my friends and fellow entertainers, who have made me proud to be an entertainer.

William Michael LeBow Stilwell
"Magic Mike" Stilwell

October 30, 2013.

Dedication

I dedicate this book to Mr. Bernie Kaye. In 1997, I went to work for Bernie Kaye's company: Entertainment Solutions West in San Diego. He was a best known agent for his professionalism, expertise, ethical values and good nature. He was more than my agent. He was a friend, my mentor and in many ways a father figure. As entertainment producers, we created special events together for over 16 years. This was a wonderful education for me.

Bernie Kaye: bandleader, entertainer and producer, has been in the entertainment business for over 50 years. Prior to that time, he worked as a night club entertainer and singer throughout the country. He did some television and radio work on the west coast then proceeded to New York where he went into the special event portion of show business.

I owe so much to this man. He has honed my skills as an entertainer, made me a better person, been at my side during some really bad stuff that happened in my life and made me a talent agent almost as good as him! Now I'm able to share all of this with you, my fellow entertainers.

Thank you, Bernie.
Mike Stilwell
November 1, 2013

Introduction

You are an entertainer. You are different. You love to make people happy. You love to see them laugh. You enjoy what you do. You like being in the spotlight. YOU ARE AN ENTERTAINER.

You may be a special entertainer such as magician, mime, juggler, comic, ventriloquist, master of ceremonies, plate spinner, vocalist, dramatic reader, caricature artist, face painter, mentalist, clown, musician, puppeteer, disc jockey, balloon twister, hypnotist, stilt walker, dancer, character imitator (e.g., Santa, Easter Bunny), etc.

You may recognize your skill as an entertainer but you could have many questions that prevent you from being successful. For years peers asked me for advice on everything from "How do you find the place to work" to "How do I get a pay raise." I have written this book to give them a resource that will answer many of these questions.

It is my hope that this guide will help you be a successful entertainer This will give you important guidelines in a variety of work locations such as a restaurants, nightclubs, hotels, tradeshows, shopping malls, planes, boats, buses, fairs, streets, homes, schools, weddings, cocktail parties, Bar Mitzvahs, conventions, trade shows, hospitality suites, hospitals, sports events, night clubs, grand openings, senior living facilities, charity events, reunions, (birthday, holiday, company) parties or a basket in hot air balloons

This book is a compressive review of things you need to know about being a professional entertainer. It will not answer all of your questions, but it will give you a good start. When I started being an entertainer there were no comprehensive guide books that I could find to help me. I have tried to include special guidelines for important topics such as marketing yourself, record keeping, legal issues, etc. Check the index to locate topics of specific interest. Remember you are unique and I suggest keeping notes along with my book. .

I hope this book will give you the information that I spent a lifetime learning the hard way.

Good Luck fellow entertainers.

Mike Stilwell
San Diego, CA USA
November 1, 2013

Contents

Chapter 1

GETTING STARTED

Do Your Research

You want to be a professional entertainer such as juggler, dancer, disc jockey, comic, magician, vocalist, musician, stilt walker, master of ceremony, palm reader, mentalist, caricaturist, character artist, face painter, psychic, clown, voice over, hypnotist, ventriloquist, balloon twister, sign twister, plate spinners, puppeteer, look-a-like, mime, etc.

To locate other entertainers or job opportunities in your field you can Google from any geographical location and see what turns up. Also, you can look in the local yellow pages. Research is very important for the success of any performer and performance.

The key to being a successful entertainer is to be different than the other person. STAND OUT! There were 25 working magicians in San Diego and I decided to create a completely different look. Most magicians wore a black and white tuxedo or a business suit. I wear an all black Zoot suit from the 30's, a colorful silk tie with playing cards on it, spats, and a black fedora hat with a small red feather to match my tie.

As I walk into any room I'm noticed immediately. In restaurants people will not ask me for coffee or, "can you get me a fork". Look at your competition and change the way you perform and the way you look.

Many times people don't remember my name, but they do remember that I'm the guy that wears all black and is very mysterious.

When they describe me to an agent or another performer they know who they are talking about. Do your research. Also think about your stage name and stand out. I know a street entertainer by the name of Jimmy Talksalot and a comic by the name of Rus T Nailz or a Magician by the name of Sleeveless.

If I know the name of the company I'm working for I research that company, learn a few facts and tie in my magic to fit in with some related information. I do a rope trick called "Professors Nightmare" which uses 3 ropes of different lengths, but they all end up being the same length. Recently I was working for a company that manufactured solar panels for homes. Here's the pitch:

Your customers have a long list of needs (I show long rope) But only have a short amount of funds (show short rope) and all you want to do with the XYZ Company is create a happy medium (show medium piece of rope). With The XYZ Company we gather all these things together with our top notch staff of engineers and create an understanding of what your needs and wants are, (now I show all three ropes are equal) That's our magic at The XYZ Company.

I know a piano player that researches a company and finds the city and state it is from and during his performance he plays the fight song for their college football team. I always ask if anyone has a birthday and do something special just for them. If you're a musician you could say "will everyone join in and sing happy birthday for so and so." I have a little birthday magic trick where some pieces of gift wrap are torn up and I restore it into a little birthday hat for the special guest.

Stage Name.

You want a name they will remember. You need something more than just your name that says what you do or what you're about. It's like naming a company. Mike Stilwell doesn't say "magician" Robert John doesn't say Mr. D.J.

I had a few fun names over the years such as Mike the Magnificent, Bumper the Baffling Bunny, and Magic Mike Stilwell. Magic Mike stuck and has been my name since I was 40. If you are really good you will be remembered no matter what your name is. Famous movie stars had stage names. Marilyn Monroe was born Norma Jean Mortenson. I have a friend that's a magician that goes by the name of "sleeveless" and another that goes by Mr. Magic.

What Makes you Special and Remarkable

Think of other entertainers.

What makes you remember them?

What makes you want to see them again?

Is it their special outfit, hair, speech, posture, or theme song?

I am a magician and I have a special signature trick that customers remember.

This is one of the many tricks I perform:

The Birthday Card trick (card on ceiling)

This trick was just one of the reasons people came back year after year. I tell a birthday person to write Happy Birthday and their name and date, and place that card in the deck. I would place the deck of cards in its box and tell the birthday person to put the deck somewhere special and after they paid their bill to ask the waitress to find me. What happens next is very magical. I take them to a different part of the restaurant and tell the birthday person who wrote on the card to get the deck from its hiding place and take the deck out of the box and find the card they wrote on. To their amazement the card is not in the deck. At that point I say, "This is Your Birthday Card." TRICK! Then I ask everyone to look up at the ceiling and there is the card with Happy Birthday and the date. I retrieve the deck of cards as I receive my applause and the guests leave with a wonderful birthday memory. What's great about this trick is that they tend to bring their friends back and show them their card and tell their version of what happened. At a local diner I had thousands of cards on the ceiling.

Your Booking Sheet/Invoice

Here are some ideas from my booking sheet. You should tailor it for your particular needs.

Essential information:

Date communication received

Date communication returned by you
Name of person who contacted you. (Previous client?)
Agent (circle yes or no)
Name of company, address, phone number, e-mail.
Private party (circle yes or no) address, phone number, e-mail.
Type of event: birthday, wedding, etc.
Type of entertainment requested – Theme?
Costumes requested – type and color.
Date, time, and place of requested entertainment.
Directions to location.
Place/venue - is it confirmed by contract?
Ages of audience.
Name of persons to be honored.
Space- Indoor, outdoor, dressing room.
What is budgeted?
Any music or other entertainers at this event.

If the contact person/client wishes to proceed then complete an invoice which may include the following information:

Each invoice should be numbered. I use a number that corresponds to the date of the event as follows:

If the event is September 19, 2013 my invoice number would be 091913. If more than one event is scheduled for the same day, letters could be added at the end to differentiate between them.

Have entertainer and client signed a contract for the services?
Have you included price, deposit, cancellation and refunds.
Additional entertainer's expenses.

Services Provided by the Client

There are additional services provided by the client, not you as the entertainer. Often I will be hired to do an after dinner magic show. When I write up the contract I will write "sound system and microphone is to be provided by the client". When you arrive at the event there should be a sound system with a microphone for you to use. If you need a microphone stand then you need to add that as well. I once had that in my contract and the client had forgotten to order it. When I arrived there was no sound system and I reminded them that they were responsible. Some entertainers provide their own sound system. I know a hypnotist that brings his own microphone.

A hypnotist may write up his contract like this:

A 60 minute comedy hypnotic show by John Doe will happen on June 3, 2014 for the XYZ Company at the MOP Hotel in the ABC room from 7:00 PM to 8:00 PM. The cost of these services is $1200.00. A reservation fee of $600.00 is to be sent with this signed contract, the balance is due the night of the event. The client is to provide 20 chairs and a sound system with (1) hand held microphone.

If the client agrees to everything on the contract they will sign it and mail it back to you.

Calendar

Knowing exactly the schedule that you are already committed to is important at all times, Should clients request your services for a particular date and time you must be able to respond immediately. If you are busy you inform them that you are in the middle of something and will call back shortly. Entertainers must determine what calendar system is best for them. This could be a digital device or a date book. It may also be advisable to have your schedule on a wall calendar at home that other family members will have access to. When scheduling your time be sure to remember any personal events you may have such as graduations and weddings.

Risk Taking

Don't be afraid of failure. Take a risk. When you are self employed there is a certain amount of risk taking. It's different from being in your comfort zone of a 9 to 5 job that pays for your 401, health care, sick days, vacation time, etc. When self employed you are responsible for your own health and dental insurance. There are no sick days. Vacations have to be planned months in advance, usually during times of the year that are not usually desirable like January and February. When I worked at a restaurant Tuesday and Wednesday nights I would plan my vacations to leave Thursday morning and return Monday Night. Everything you do is a risk. If I have someone else fill in for me while I'm on vacation there is a risk that the guests will be prefer him/her to me or owner will like him/her better. They could possibly do a bad job which would reflect on my reputation just because I wanted some time off.

Risk is like juggling, you don't want to take too many risks at a time, so don't have too many balls in the air. Take little steps. You may talk to many people before you get a desirable gig. You could be a fantastic classical guitar player, and may do a dozen auditions before that country club or hotel hires you. They may hire you for a month which may result in a 10 year steady and so every Friday to Saturday you are doing what you love. The client may then decide to not have a live band or entertainment. It's all a risk.

I was booked for a "trial time of 90 days". It looked like a perfect gig. I turned down future work that was on the same days that I was working the club. On the 90th day I was told they are going to discontinue entertainment for a while. I then went to the big boss and gave reasons why he still needed me. I explained that during my 90 day trial period I created a following and made the guests wait time seem shorter. I even helped the servers turn over the tables. I told him I am a good fit and have helped business. By stepping up and taking a risk I kept my job for another 2 years.

Get out there. Your phone is not going to ring if no one knows you exist. Always carry business cards, talk to everyone, and pass out your card to everyone you meet. Do as many charity events as you can and get letters from them for references. They are not going to say, Mike came and entertained for free the other night. They are going to say Mike entertained at our fundraiser and helped us meet our goal. Thank You Mike.

Take risks. Taking risks is an important part of being a professional entertainer.

Agents:

Booking agents, talent agents, entertainment producers, personal managers

There are several ways to obtain bookings. You can proceed on your own, be hired by an agent, or obtain referrals from satisfied customers. I will mention some of my experiences with agents:

When I was in the Navy I met three wonderful agents. Bill Green's Music used to book me at the world famous Del Coronado Hotel. Bill was a Big Band leader and a talent agent. He always gave me sound advice and told me to arrive at my gigs at least 30 minutes prior to show time. This meant leaving my house 2 hours before show time because of possible traffic and parking problems.

One time I forgot my shoes and as I was walking into the Del Coronado Hotel about an hour before show time I was met by Bill Green, He said "Mike you look great, white top hat, white tail coat, white pants, black and white vest, white shirt, white tie, oops. "BROWN LOAFERS". Oh my, what should I do?" Bill said you don't have time to go home as the show starts in 30 minutes. I had been doing a beautiful dove act and as a surprise to Bill I thought a white tuxedo would be great for the hotel. Bill said "You have 3 options, you can go in the gift shop and buy a $60.00 pair of black shoes, or you could go on stage in just your black socks, or you could stop by the shoe shine man and have him cover your brown loafers with black polish" That's exactly what I did. I never had those shoes changed back to brown as a reminder to pay attention to every detail. Practical advice from an agent can alert you to unforeseen situations.

Another wonderful agent was Jim Deacy who had Bud and Kelley Melcher and Loren Smith in his office. Jim taught me how to work tradeshows, hospitality suites, hotels, convention centers, and the destination management companies. He told me, "Whenever you are on an **agent gig**, never pass out your own business card. Remember when you are on one of my jobs refer them to the host of the party. If they ask for a card never pass out your own card. It's amazing how many entertainers don't understand that small request or the ethics behind it. The entertainer would not be at this event if it weren't for the agent.

One time I was working on a job that needed 3 other magicians. It was a job where four magicians were hired by the agent, the agent was hired by the destination manager, and the destination manager was hired by an incentive company out of New York. The incentive company was hired by the client, a well known copy machine company. I was told to tell my magicians not to pass anyone's card, not yours, not your agents, no one's card". I told my magicians "The Client has requested that we not pass any of our cards or the agents cards." After the entertainment everything seemed fine.

The next morning the phone rang at about 10 am, ""Mike, this is the agent from last night. Could you please come down to my office?' At the office my agent showed me a business card. I recognized it is as the card of one of the magicians I had hired. To test the integrity of their company someone asked one of my magicians for a business card. They enticed him by saying they wanted to cut out the middle man and make him the official magician for their company. My magician was set up. I turned the card over and there were 5 initials on the back, everyone's hands that the card was passed to until it got to my agents hands. My jaw hit the table, I wanted an explanation. The agent wanted an explanation so I called the magician and asked how it went last night, he said fine. I said you are on speaker phone because you owe us an explanation for why you gave out one of your cards after I told you not to. He said he knew it was wrong, but that all he saw were dollar signs for being that company's magician. I asked that he write my agent a letter of apology but he never did. That agent never used us again, and I never called that magician again. I'm sure my agent lost the account with the company because one entertainer was unethical and did not follow the rules.

Having a Personal Manager is another option. As you become more successful you may be just too busy entertaining to do all the other necessary work such as: negotiating contracts, arranging travel, hotel, ground transportation, back line, promotions, marketing, etc.

This is when you may want to consider finding a personal manager who assumes those responsibilities and including your income. One that I have used is David Belenzon, owner of David Belenzon Management, Inc. who represents many highly successful entertainers such as Mime Mark Wenzel, Ventriloquist Keven Johnson, Juggler Michael Moschen,, Mentalist Magician Max Maven, The Kingston Trio, Karen Mason, and

Chinese Acrobats. However, he has some smaller venues that he saves for local talent and has used me for over 25 years.

Later as I progressed in my career I was an outside contractor (1994-2013) and was responsible for providing over 150 acts for the operations manager at the San Diego Zoo.

One example was the "Night Time Zoo." program for which I contracted many single entertainers to do acts that were scattered around different parts of the zoo. In addition I contracted for a major stage production.

David Belenzon was contracted by me to provide acrobats, script, music, sound, and lights, for a wonderful stage production that was part of the total entertainment package that we co- produced for the San Diego 73 day summer "Night Time Zoo." David's' entertainers performed for 3 summers to a sold out crowd at the 1500 seat outdoor theater.

In 1997 I went to work for Bernie Kaye, San Diego's best known agent recognized for his wonderful ethics and professional reputation. He has been my friend and father figure in so many ways. I worked with Bernie's company, Entertainment Solutions West, Inc as an entertainment producer and as of 2013 we have created special events together for 16 years. What an education for me.

Bernie Kaye, bandleader, entertainer, and producer is president of this organization. He has been in this particular phase of the entertainment business for over 50 years. Prior to that time he worked his act as a night club entertainer singing in

`night spots throughout the country. He did some radio and television work on the west coast and then in New York City where he did the special event portion of show business

I owe so much to this man. He has honed my skills as an entertainer and made me a better person during some really bad periods of my life. He taught me to be like him as a talent agent with the ethics and reputa-tion that are so important. I'm going to pass these important things on to you.

This is a brief description of the roles of a personal management company. Of course you would need to consider your decisions carefully when selecting personal managers since they will be making numerous significant decisions for you.

Stay Busy

I know that I have said this before, but Stay Busy!

The worst thing that can happen to you as an entertainer is for management to see you not working and standing around chatting with the staff. Stay busy entertaining the guests. On slow nights you must pace yourself more slowly but at the same time you should not forget anyone. If you promise to go to a table that has requested you, and they were eating when you arrived, then you MUST make it back later to that table.

Business Cards

I can't tell you how many times I've asked entertainers for a business card, and they couldn't come up with one. Always have a card. Your next gig may come from that request. I have tricks that ensure that the card gets in the clients hands. At one time I printed on the other side of the card: "Appearing at the Corvette Diner every Tuesday and Wednesday night". I would not put the times so the guests would call the restaurant to find out what time I was coming in. This created interest and talk among the employees. I also kept a business card next to the telephone where I worked so the host person could find my number in case a guest called wanting to hire me for a private party.

It is important to read the section on <u>AGENT</u> describing when not to distribute your card.

Status

Are you and amateur, semi professional or professional entertainer?

Amateur entertainers are usually hobbyists and are not paid for their services. They do it for the love of performing. Semi professional entertainers usually have another full time job and do part time entertaining on the side and are paid for their services. While I was in the Navy I did children magic shows and corporate events on the weekends. If you are a full time professional entertainer all of your income comes from entertaining. This is your livelihood. It's a hard road to take and is how you pay your bills. I have found that you also need to do some things that are related to your craft. I'm a professional magician that entertains at parties most of the time. I also teach magic privately and manufacture specific magic tricks for magic shops. I make some custom magic props for other magicians. Remember to check any laws that relate to income taxes, liability, government registration requirements, etc.

Holidays and Odd Hours

Most entertainers are working when other people are on holiday or after working hours. This also includes working nights. They work weekends at the company picnic, the mall, and usually every holiday there will be some entertainment. If you don't want to work holidays or odd hours, then you probably won't be a professional entertainer. Remember, the client sets the time and place you will work.

Opinions

It is important to ask for opinions good or bad which is what we must do to succeed.

I was working with a magic show dressed up as a big rabbit named Bumper the Baffling Bunny. I thought I had a near perfect show and character. It was very early in my career and I invited Mike Rogers, a very well known professional magician, author, and consultant to see one of my magic shows at a local fair. Opinions are not always good news. I thought I was going to impress him. Instead he tore my act apart. Mike was also a good friend and I just assumed that he would sugar coat the show and the character. He proceeded to tell me that I was not a rabbit doing a magic show but some guy dressed in a rabbit costume trying to do a magic show. "You need to figure out how to see out of the costume and you should wear black makeup under the rabbit head so that children do not see the guy inside. You need to learn tricks that you are comfortable doing in gloves. You need to read about rabbits and their antics, and work on this character". Later that day I went into hiding for 6 months and worked on the aspects that Mike suggested. When I was ready I met with Mike again and we recreated a rabbit that did magic. This was the only costumed character to become a member of Hollywood's famous Magic Castle.

Passport

You may never need a passport, but if you get a call you should be prepared.

I had a call from an agent to fill in for a world famous magician that was sick with the flu in Japan. It was a 4 day gig that paid for 7 days, which included all the travel, hotel, food, a translator and ground transportation to and from the event. I couldn't go, I didn't have a passport. I do now.

Finding Your Talent

We were all created to be different. Some people have specific talents to be doctors, teachers, firefighters, pastors and entertainers just to name a few.

In the beginning of your journey to be an entertainer it's hard and exciting at the same time. You may have a day job and start to do what you absolutely love to do as a hobby. You may find that people will actually pay for this hobby that you love so much you would be willing to do for free. You may still be in school and find that working for tips at a local park, making balloon animals for the kids, or playing the guitar is very lucrative.

When I was in the Navy I did magic shows and was a magic bartender on weekends and some week days which is hard to do when you have a day job. I thought that I was making almost as much money working Friday, Saturday and Sunday as I did in the Navy for the whole week. However, I didn't consider the military benefits like, health care, dental care, and cost of living. I was only looking at the dollars and comparing the paychecks. Be extremely careful, especially if you have a wife and children. Don't be quick to give up that steady income for a possible chance to be a successful entertainer as it doesn't happen overnight. Sometimes being at the right place at the right time does work for a very few entertainers. Most of them have to work hard on their craft.

In my case, I'm known in my city, but not outside of my city. I've been an entertainer for 80% of my life. I'm not going to sugar coat it, it's not easy.

One time I was performing with Steve Allen, world famous talk show host, comedian, writer, song writer, and musician. We were sitting in the green room waiting to go on and I was the opening for Steve Allen. I was scared to death. I asked Steve, "How do you go from doing casuals and small rooms to working in the main showroom of Vegas." Then he said, "What makes you think that you have arrived just because you worked a showroom in Vegas?" He went on to say" "A lot of guys are starving who have been in those showrooms." He said "Everyone has a different success story and you will know yours when it happens". Then I asked Steve "Do you have any advice on raising children?" Steve said as he chuckled," Never raise unless you have jacks or better". Just then I heard my introduction from the M.C. and I never got a chance to chat with Steve Allen again.

Privacy

As you move to become a professional entertainer you will need to determine ways to protect your privacy. Remember to keep all of your personal information such as telephone number, home address, website, and legal name separate from your business information. As an example you can use your stage name and get an additional website and PO Box for your business. Present technology makes it possible to obtain much personal information.

Be careful of the personal information you give to others. It's easy to get caught up in the moment when you have many people around you after a performance. Always be aware of those around you. Creating a following of people that come to see you every week is much different than a stalker.

Lead Sheets

I obtain 75% of my work from repeat customers which may only be 25% of the clients on my list. I'm always working my lead sheet. My lead sheet is a form that I make in house. A computer program may be used to record this information or card files could also be used.

On a typical lead sheet I specify Client Name, Phone No., Date Last Worked, Cost, and Occasion. I also make note of when I last called and response received. I make up this form as I go through past bookings a few months ahead. These records assist me to remind customers of my availability. For example, if your lead sheet has a record that you gave a previous birthday party for XYZ on a specific date you could send a reminder a few months ahead of his next birthday indicating you would be available for his next party. You could mention the theme for the last party and suggest another theme for this one. I will call for December jobs in September.

I sometimes go back 2-3 years on my lead sheets and check my status so I know what was said. Most of my work comes from the few clients that use me over and over. I may do 150 to 200 shows a year, 25 % are one time shows, 25% will be kids shows, 25% will be agent gigs with some repeat, 15 % are fundraiser/benefits, and 10% are donations for silent auctions, benefits or churches. Some time ago I was doing 300 performances a year. If clients ask to call them back in the summer or later that year I highlight the information on my lead sheet, and contact them. It usually pays off.

I have booking /lead sheets that go back 25 years. I had a client tell me that their son was getting married in the same house that the parents were. I did magic at their wedding 22 years ago. I asked the client what the date of their wedding was, and while I was talking to him, I looked at the booking sheet and casually said. "Do you still live at 524 5th Ave.?" and he said, "Oh my Gosh. You still know the address." They had just moved out of that house a few weeks earlier, but he was impressed that I had records that went t back that far.

I keep my booking sheets in case I go back and entertain there again. I make notes of what routines I did and what I wore. A musician or band leader will make notes of what songs they sang and so on.

Military Service

While you are in the military you can hone your craft during down time. I leaned most of my card tricks during those long 6 month deployments. If you play a loud musical instrument you may want to wait until you are on shore to practice. But if you have another talent while in the military service which in my case the Navy, they really liked that I was a magician. It was great for moral. I entertained for the sick at hospitals, retirement homes, and recruitment fair. I did a magic show in my tuxedo for a group of students and when I returned to the stage in my uniform the students were surprised that I was in the Navy.

It was like magic when someone told me I had orders to squadron HSL-35 Code name "The Magicians." This is an example of how in various ways you can get started in your entertainment skills.

Stage Fright

Nervousness before or during a performance best describes stage fright. I use to be nauseated before each show. Now I can't wait to get on stage. I know someone that does 50 jumping jacks before he goes on to do stand- up comedy. A friend of mine who plays violin in The San Diego City Orchestra reads a book just before show time. Another buddy of mine prays. As a rule I never eat a heavy meal before show time.

Everyone in show business deals with this in their own way

Keeping Track of your Schedule

Find a system that allows you to follow your schedule and don't forget to remember the "Hold" dates. There are numerous digital devices that will assist you to keep track of your schedules. Some may still prefer pocket calendars, giant wall calendars, or other hand written methods. Remember you're booking sheets and invoices will also provide additional information.

Hold Date

You have agreed with your client to hold a specific date for an event. See the section on "Fees for Service" for additional information related to this. To avoid confusion make sure that all parties have signed an agreement. You must not schedule another event on the date you have placed on hold. Should you get a call to do a different gig for the same date from another person I will call Jane, your date book will note that you have a "hold" from Entertainment Solutions for a company picnic. What do you do? You say to Jane "I have a hold from one of my agents in San Diego for a picnic from 12-4, let me find out if the "hold" is good or not. Please give me 24 hours to call my agent and I will call you back and let you know if I can do your party" This is known as "Honoring the Hold" and giving your client on hold the first "24 hours of refusal". You can call your agent and tell him "I received a call to do a July 4th 2013 for a gig from 2-4 PM which I have on hold. Are you using me or can I take this other job?" This will force the agent to call his client for a decision in 24 hours. The agent may say you are released and can now tell Jane that you are available to do her party

If you are not booked by an agent you would make the call directly to your client. If you get a reputation for not honoring holds, agents and event planners will not call you. I know many entertainers who do not honor "holds" They don't work very often.

Branding

This is a new expression created by the marketing folks. You must Brand your services. Branding is what separates you from your competition. It's what your clients and future customers expect from you. It's a promise to deliver what you say and do.

Branding is your identity. I think of it as a talking label. It's what separates you from the other entertainers. Show me or prove to me why I should hire you. Why do your new clients call on your services, what makes them think of you? Why use your services? In my case I believe my identity and my persona is why folks are attracted to me and my profession. When I walk into a room people usually know who I am by the way I look. I'm the guy that wears a long black coat, spats on his shoes, a fedora and a bright tie and has a smooth as silk voice and is charming and entertaining. I'm reliable, affordable, a great value, and memorable. They will be talking about me long after the cake is eaten. You must create the reason your clients search you out and hire you. Why do your clients and prospected clients think of you?

There are many professional magicians in San Diego and that's a lot of competition. I've created knish markets where I'm the only one the customer will think of, or be recommended by an agent or a party planner. I'm the Bar/Bat Mitzvah magician that performs during the cocktail hour of the Bar or Bat Mitzvahs. When I was first learning how to do Mitzvahs I had no idea what I was doing, so I consulted a Rabbi. Every time I had a question Rabbi Martin Lawson would advise me and answer my questions. He took time to encourage me and be the best that I could be.

I began doing magic for children, adults, and history making events where relatives and friends have not seen each other for a long time. I'm a founding member of the largest event service association that specialize in adding the right vendor for your Bar and Bat Mitzvahs. We have a roster for the Mitzvah family to look at and know that we are qualified to entertain at their event. In 2012 we celebrated our 10 year anniversary as Jewish Event Specialist and the directory has over 70 venders. We have caterers, live music, decor and event planners, disc jockeys, activities and amusements, Invitations/Judaica, photography, video, and venues. We began with 10 venders that met at Bar and Bat Mitzvahs. We have a code of ethics, a mission statement, and membership requirements. We are known as BESA, Bar/Bat Mitzvah Event Services Association. Our "Branding" for BESA is knowing that you will have the best qualified vender to provide the services for a very special and history making event.

Check us out www.besasandiego.com. It's not easy to become a BESA Member. It really means something to a client when you tell them that you are a member of BESA. The clients have an ease and trust of knowing that they don't have to worry if the vender will be on time or will eat from the clients buffet (unless invited). They are confident we are the best at what we do. Each year we have our own trade show called the BESA Expo, It runs 12-5 on a Sunday and we invite everyone that is planning some kind of Simcha (special event).

On The Job Training

Most of what I knew in the Navy was because of OJT. Sure we read books, even went to specialty schools and leaned a lot of information in Boot Camp. But nothing can beat good old fashion "On the Job Training".

By this I mean getting out there and doing it, right or wrong, and learning from your mistakes. However it is important to practice your skills prior to appearing before an audience. This is one of the reasons I wanted to write a book. To help others reduce their mistakes. It's alright to make some but it is my hope that my book will keep you on track and focused.

It's not OK to go to a job unprepared. I have seen some magicians go to a magic shop, buy a new trick, read the directions on the way to the show, and do the trick for the first time. This is not OJT, this is stupid. I will be at an event doing all my "A" material and tell the audience "would you like to see something new that I'm working on?" It may not work, but the only way I can really practice this effect is with a live audience.

The audience loves helping you perfect a new routine. Comics especially need an audience to try out new material, and they do a lot of "non-paid" open mike nights at local comedy clubs to try them out. This is the best form of OJT. Hypnotists have it the hardest as every show must be a form of OJT. When dealing with many people it is difficult for them to predict how the show will turn out until the end. I admire their showmanship and their presentation which is all unrehearsed. When they have new people on stage no one knows what's going to happen next. The first 20 or 30 shows must be difficult until they get into a rhythm and routine that an entertainer hopes will take place during the show. A caricature artist will eventually run out of family members and friends to draw but he will learn much more by sitting in a park and drawing strangers for tips. I once entertained people at bus stops with new card tricks, magic routines, or even stupid jokes I was working on, I'm still amazed that those people still talk to me.

Background Check

If you are booked for a gig by an agency, company, or others, they may have special requirements in addition to recognizing your special form of entertainment. These might include background checks, health insurance, flu shots. Etc. Remember that all information you shared on Facebook and other social media could become public knowledge. Perhaps you may want to do a background search on yourself to be aware of what information about you is available to others. There are numerous companies that will conduct background searches for a modest fee.

Changes - Moving, Phone Numbers, E-Mail Addresses

Moving? Have a new Phone Number? A new E Mail Address?

One of the biggest complaints that agents have is when entertainers don't notify them when they move. A serious problem can arise when a check is sent to an entertainer and the entertainer doesn't get the check all because the agent didn't provide his changed address. Make out a post card notifying all your clients that employ you on a regular basis (agents, party planners, event producers and so on) and mail it to them. Do not rely on a phone call. Also e-mail them the changes. Many e- mails fall through the crack or get deleted by mistake.

Do not be assured that your mail will be forwarded. It will be forwarded for a short time and then either it will be returned to the sender or left in a dead file. I've seen contracts and checks that did not get to the entertainer because he forgot to tell the booker that he had a new address. Also, if there is a change in your show format, a new web site, or anything that has been changed concerning you the entertainer, always let the person(s) that book your services know.

A good example of this is that many bookers, like catering companies, will have a vender profile that gives them information about you and your needs when they are referring you to their client. The profile will show what you do and how much it costs. I was recently called by a person from a catering company to do a 30 minute family fun magic show. I did shows for this company for over 25 years but this was a new sales person. They always had a small sound system and sometimes a stage at these events for me. About 90% of these events are outside and most are company picnics.

For the last gig I did for them they only had a microphone on a stand and it was hard to do my show without the use of both of my hands. I mentioned this to the sales person that had called me for the show. "Can I get a head set this time instead of a mike with a stand?" She said "I don't see in your profile that you need a microphone and sound system"

You will need to provide that for this show" I said that in my 25 years of working for your company I have never provided a sound system. It was later discovered that her client had a sound system at the event to make announcements. My profile now reads "Client to provide sound system and wireless microphone for magic show"

As a marketing tool I send out a post card every couple of years, one to remind them that I'm still available and two, to let them verify that they have all of my correct information.

Chapter 2

FEES FOR SERVICE AND RECORDS

Prices

It's 2013 in San Diego. A client calls and wants a quote. Here are some average prices for entertainers in San Diego. These prices will be different at other locations and can vary $25.00 to $50.00. If you live in the Midwest prices for a caricature artist may be quite lower than in New York.

These prices are direct from entertainers.

Face Painter $75.00 to $100.00 per hour, Balloon twister $75.00 to $100.00 per hour, Caricature Artist and Psychics (palm reader, tarot) $100.00 to $150.00 per hour, Magician $150.00 to 250.00 per hour, Harpist $175.00 to $225.00 per hour, Piano, Keyboard, or Guitarist $125.00 to $175.00 per hour. Stilt walker $125.00 to $200.00 per hour, Santa with a fake beard $75.00 to $100.00 per hour, a Real Beard Santa $125.00 to $175.00 per hour. Clowns in full costume $125.00 to $175.00 per hour,. Look-a-likes (people that look like someone famous) $250.00 to $500.00 per hour for meet and greet. Bands have a different price schedule, depending on the number of musicians and type of band. They usually have a 3 or 4 hour minimum. D.J.'s usually have a 4 hour minimum on weekends and a 2 hour minimum during the week.

Some offer karaoke and music for $150.00 to $250.00 per hour. Some D.J.'s offer complete light and special effects with music and these prices can be over $2000.00.

How Much to Charge

Let's say you play violin really well and you have decided that you want to play at weddings on weekends to supplement your income or just for fun. I have found that the entertainers that only want to have fun and don't care how much they make really hurt the professional entertainers that are trying to make a living. In my industry there are a lot of "hobbyists" that have good paying day jobs and just like to do a casual party here and there for a very cheap rate. My thought is that if you want to play at your talent do it in a way that will not affect the livelihood of professional or semi professional entertainers

When I was starting to charge for my magic shows in my early teens, I made 3 x 5 cards and printed "Kids Magic Shows, $50.00" and added my name

and phone number. I placed these everywhere that parents would see them: laundromats, supermarkets, and the library. In my 20's, as a supplement to my day job, I was able to charge $100.00 and I was advertizing in the yellow pages under "Entertainment". Years later when I decided to be a full time magician the rate for a Birthday Party Magician was $150.00 for a 30-40 minute show. By 2013 the rate in San Diego was $185.00 to $225.00 for the same show.

The best way to find out what to charge for your services is to do some homework. You cannot call another entertainer and ask what they charge because they are not going to tell you. They don't want the competition and they don't want you to know their pricing. Be creative to find out what others are charging.

Perhaps a friend who is planning a wedding next year could make a call as follows:

"Hi, I'm Heather, and I'm going to have a wedding next year, don't have a date yet but I want to gather some information" Please tell me about your services. They probably will respond.

There are prices you will charge a client when you are booked by an agent, producer of entertainment, wedding planner, event planner, and anyone that re- sells entertainment. An agent has to resell or add a commission to the sale of your services. As a rule entertainers have a "wholesale "rate for the agent that is 25-50% lower than you would charge the client if they called you instead of the agent. I suggest you should spend time with your agent or other sellers of entertainment.

Talent Agent

A talent agent is also known as a booking agent and represents entertainers that are available for hire for all types of special events. Talent agents not only represent entertainers but also models, athletes, writers, and actors. Most Talent agents are licensed and bonded in their state and carry a 2 million dollar insurance policy. (Presently most entertainers must also carry the same policy)

Wherever you live, it is important for you to do your research related to all entertainment agencies in your areas. There is great variety from very small to large organizations.

As you are more successful you may be getting gigs from influential agencies that are more comprehensive and include celebrities as clients. If you are fortunate to get a small gig as part of a full production show or event with a famous agency such as Bollotta Entertainment in San Diego, CA, be aware that in addition to your fee for service you may have experiences that would contribute to your growth

Tips

I saw a balloon twister at a restaurant with a button on his jacket that said "Tipping" is not a city in China!"

For many years I would walk away from customers offering tips. Sometimes parents would come to my table as they were leaving and put something in my pocket. This would start a chain reaction from table to table. I never wanted a guest feeing obligated to tip the performer.

Sometimes a guest would say" Can you make this disappear" as they held up a bill. I created a trick just for that. I would ask them to roll it like a cigarette and place it in my fist. I would push it down and have them say "GO! "At that point I would open my hand and the bill would have vanished. There are many restaurant entertainers that work tips into their routine hoping to get them at the end.

I knew a magician that would ask a guest for a $10.00 bill. He then tore the bill in half and let the guest keep one piece. An orange is produced, cut open, and the other half of the bill is inside. It matched exactly the piece the guest is holding. While this is a great trick the bill is now wet and gooey as the magician leaves it on a table. Usually the guest will say thank you, please keep it. I do a similar trick with a card that is torn up and the guest keeps a piece. Then I ask the guest to hand me a sugar packet from a bowl of sugar and inside the sugar packet is the playing card with the missing piece. (Thanks to magicians Mike Rogers and Terry Lunceford for helping me with the routine).

Remember that tips are income and make sure to keep records for filing your tax return.

Discounts

A discount is a reduction to the regular price.

I give a 10% discount for fellow entertainers and to my repeat clients. I give the government a 2% discount if they pay me in 15 days instead of the usual 30 days. They pay all discounted invoices first so it's worth taking a little less to help with my cash flow. For some charitable organizations that are having a fundraiser, I give a 50% discount.

Payment Methods

Be prepared to accept various methods of payment. Modern technology can provide fast methods to pay with hand held devices. Credit cards require special equipment for each type. Other methods may include cash, check, money order, or bank transfer. If you are unable to accept a particular form of payment you could lose a gig.

Getting Paid and Collection Problems

If you follow the guidelines previously addressed in the sections related to Getting Started, Booking, Invoices, and Contracts you should have few problems. It is very important to have a written agreement/contract signed by both client and entertainer concerning how much, when, and how payments are to be made. Of course this will vary with your situation.

SOME PROBLEMS YOU MAY HAVE
During your gig your client places a cash/check payment in your pocket. Since other people are present it is not appropriate to count it at this time.
The payment received is not correct.
The date on the check is incorrect.
The payment received is too small or too large.
The check is not signed.
The credit card payment was not honored.
Your name on the check is incorrect.
The payment is not received when due.
The check bounces

WHAT CAN YOU DO
Always count the payment that was placed in your pocket in front of the client.
When a problem is identified, notify your client as soon as possible.
If the problem is not resolved immediately, follow up with correspondence including a copy of the signed agreement/contract and an invoice.
When using mailed correspondence have the envelope certified with a required return receipt specified.

WHEN ALL EFFORTS FAIL
You can hire a collection agency.
Hire an attorney.
If the cost, effort, and stress are more than the amount owed then file it as an income tax loss. This is a client you will not work for again.

Also note in your personal memory bank as a lesson learned and refuse to it make you a negative unhappy entertainer.

CAUTION
Do not harass your client.
Do not threaten your client.
Be professional and inform your client of your plans to collect.
Use Small Claims Court.
Research local government rules for your area.

Barter Services

I have a file of barter services. During a bad economy people love to trade services. I've had my car repaired, limo services, hotel rooms, plumber help, painting, printing for my business cards and other marketing supplies, massages, and dinners in the finest restaurants in the city. I place an ad every couple of months on craigslist.com. It's free and I say "Magician Looking to Trade Value $200.00 per hour. What have you got for trade?"

Last December I did a major hotel's employee party during the holidays for 2 hours and as a trade I got a dinner for two in the hotel restaurant, a $250.00 room, and breakfast for two the next day. The party was Sunday afternoon and I considered it a great deal. A while ago I did a party for a car dealership and in exchange they fixed a broken part. You must remember to follow your IRS guidelines to record and report the value of services received.

Fringe Benefits

This applies to working at a restaurant. After working at a restaurant for a couple of years, and having received a raise or two, there may be a time when they can't afford to give you a raise but will make it up in "fringe benefits".

In addition to your wage, the employer, manager, or owner may offer you a free meal instead of paying half price for your food. Sometimes my employer paid for my business cards, tent cards for the tables, and give-a-ways that I gave to children.

One time the Corvette Diner owner printed 10,000 Pogs. Magic Mike had his own Pog. This was a children's game similar to marbles. One year parking was so bad that the employer gave me my own parking spot behind the restaurant marked "Magic Mike". After working at the Corvette Diner restaurant for 10 years the owners gave me a 3 day, 2 nights stay in Las Vegas.

While working at Houlihan's restaurant the management gave me a bar tab for $25.00. Since many people were waiting to see me during Sunday brunch I would buy them a beverage of their choice while they were waiting for a table. This was great public relations for me as their entertainer and also good for the restaurant. After a few minutes I would come back and entertain them.

Charities Benefits and Fund Raisers

When you are new to the entertainment field you will be doing many free shows just for the publicity. Always ask for a letter from the organization that you had entertained for free. They usually don't mention that you donated your services but they enjoyed your services. A letter of appreciation on letter head looks great.

I have two hard and fast rules: The first is that if I'm asked to give my services for a local charity and the event is for children with life threatening illnesses and the money goes directly to the children, I will perform for free. If a charity calls me to an event where everyone is donating their time and no one is paid, then I too will donate.

Sometimes there's a limited budget for our services. Usually I will offer a two for one. I work for two hours and get paid for one. I may donate a free hour for a silent auction or a free private magic lesson from one of San Diego's favorite magicians. You must investigate the charity event before you talk money or freebee. I do about 25 charitable events a year, 20 of them for free and the others for a reduced rate. I only do free events for life threatening illnesses that effect children in San Diego.

One of the best "freebies" I ever did was when I was in my teens. I did a magic show for the closed circuit TV of a local hospital and at the end they showed my picture, name "Mike the Magnificent", my phone number, and that I was available for parties.

We all do free jobs. I was asked if I could go to a homeless shelter and entertain the children. My schedule was clear and I answered yes. They have no budget for entertainment, so it's your choice to make. You can always say you're not available.

When I do Santa I go to hospitals and retirement homes. One year I stopped by to give blood at a local blood bank.

Hold - Reservation Fee

I ask for a reservation fee, I'm reserving their date for the special event. I'm not taking another job for that time slot.

Usually I ask for 50% of the total and the balance the day of the event. If they cancel the event before 30 days from the event date I refund their reservation fee. If they cancel after 29 days they do not get a refund. Reservation fees should go into a separate account until show time.

Many times you will be asked to hold a specific date and time for an event. Once agreed, it is important that this date be honored and no other gig be planned.

Invoices and Records

An office supply store will have an invoice book that has carbon copies for your files. You can also use a computer program to record and distribute your letter of confirmation and invoice.

I number my invoices as follows:

If the date of the event is September 19, 2013 my invoice number would be 091913. If I had more than one event on the same day I would number the first 091913A and would add subsequent letters for the later ones. The invoice should include the name of the entertainer, performance description, date, time, and place. It should include what the client is to provide such as sound system, stand, microphone, etc. The total cost of the entertainer's services and the non refundable reservation fee should be specified. Clear instructions are to be written as to whom the payments are to be sent, the address, and by what method and when due.

Repeat Business

I tell people 50% of my work comes from 25% of my clients.

That's because 50% of my work is repeat business. 40% is referral from another job and 10% comes from my website and other advertizing outlets.

Repeat customers need to be rewarded for hiring you again. One way I reward my repeat clients is to charge them less than the going rate. I charge them what I charged them the last time I performed for them. As an incentive I will also add extra time as a reward for hiring me again at no additional charge. I have clients that hired me continually for 20 years. I have clients tell me" my friends won't RSVP unless they know that you're going to be there".

This is great for your ego and pocketbook. If it weren't for my repeat clients my family would have had some very lean years. The goal is to turn new clients into repeat clients. I have some clients that hire me every time they have a party. After one woman built a new pool I was hired on a hot summer day for a big pool party to celebrate. Another time her daughter had a baby and I did a baby shower. Every year I performed at her company party and summer picnic for her employees. Take care of those repeat clients.

Chapter 3

LOCATION

Scouting for a New Location

I like to hang out in places where I would like to work in the future. The venue that you want to work at doesn't know that you want to work there. In fact they don't know that they need you.

Instead of cold calling, I will stop by on a regular basis for a cup of coffee and something to eat. Often it's after a performance and I will be in my "outfit". I always sit at the bar instead of a table and will strike up a conversation with the bartender or server. Sooner or later they will ask why I'm dressed the way I am and I will tell them. If appropriate I will do a trick or tell a joke. I will become a "regular".

Each time I walk in I will be recognized as someone they know "Hi Magic Mike, soup today?" At some point I will mention that my services would work at their place and will get to know who the decision maker is. I will find out the best time to chat with them about making the customers wait time seem shorter for Sunday brunch or their "Happy Hour".

Remember, the server, the bartender and even the manager can love you, but if they are not the one making the decisions you are just spinning your wheels. If you are trying to contact a restaurant, country club or night club, determine the best time to meet with the decision maker.

Finding a new restaurant that wants your type of entertainment is not always easy. It requires lots of home work. If you play a musical instrument you may want to scout out the resorts or hotel cocktail lounges.

For me as a magician I try to find restaurants that are really busy and have long wait times. I keep notes with the name and location of the restaurant and the parking situation. I will also make several visits to determine the food, service, and customer satisfaction. You need to get a feel for what the customer may be doing while they are waiting. How long is the wait, are guests getting bored, and are they leaving because the wait is too long? You really have to see that there is a wait and assume that they need your services.

Private Homes

Frequently you may demonstrate your skills in a home setting like family birthdays, anniversaries, graduations, etc. In addition to your special preparation for a gig as described in the previous chapter, there are other things you should consider when working in a private residence.

If it's a gated community, remind the client to notify the person at the gate house that you are permitted to enter. Be considerate of your client's neighbors as to where you park, and sound levels.

This is the client's home so always ask permission for anything you may desire which may be a need for toilet facilities, place to change clothes, or getting a drink.

Be sensitive to religious and ethnic cultures. As an example it may be a custom to remove shoes when entering. Also do not occupy a room alone, especially with a child. Keep safety in mind when setting up equipment and performing.

Street Entertaining

"Busking" is where some of us started. Entertaining on streets, parks, or even in bars and shopping malls is very hard to learn. You have to stop people who are walking by, and get them to watch you entertain. You basically set up a table and entertain for 10-15 minutes, then pass the hat for tips and then move to another area.

Most places like a public park, subway stations, or shopping centers require a signup sheet or a permit to entertain on these premises. It's a tough way to make a buck, few can do it well, and others make a living at it. Sometimes this is" it"- a true test of your passion, motivation and skill.

Being able to have a great patter (dialog) is key since you must be funny with your hat lines like I used to say: "If you are local, please just drop your tip in the hat, but if you are visiting, please fold up your donation and place into the hat!"

Contact your local Chamber of Commerce and police station to see if you need a special permit instructions or license to work as a street entertainer.

Restaurants

Oh Waiter!

In most cases our mode of dress makes us look like waiters so many times a guest would ask me for more coffee or a fork and I would let the server know. But after a while when they were really busy I started answering the needs of the guests. I wanted to be a team player and I would get a fork for them, pour some coffee and even seat them. This was a mistake, this was not my job.

One day I got a letter from the boss telling me that my job is to entertain, not get coffee or seat the guests. My job is to entertain and if a guest needed something I would let the server know the table that needed them. The servers were always impressed that I knew the table numbers.

Respect your waitresses, waiters, servers, and staff.

At some restaurants the wait staff will only be concerned with the guest's need until they get to know and trust you. I always show respect for the wait staff and introduce myself. I explain that if they say "behind" as they come behind me with the tray of food I will move aside and prevent an accident. I let the wait staff know the days I work and the hours. I also make them aware that I have over 30 years experience working in restaurants as an entertainer. I like to hang out in places where I would like to work in the future. The venue that you want to work at doesn't know that you want to work there. In fact they don't know that they need you.

For the ladies I always bring a rose on Mother's Day and a red carnation on Valentine's Day. During the holidays I bring in bigger candy canes for the staff and smaller ones for the guests. Respect your wait staff. When I'm at the tables I make sure not to interrupt the server while they are talking to the guests. After I get to know them I engage them in the routines so that they are part of what's happening at their table.

When working in a restaurant you have a captive audience.

Many books have been written about how to be a better restaurant magician and other entertainers may find this helpful. My book will help people be good entertainers.

Other books on the topic of working restaurants and bars are:

Table Hopping by Bruce Postgate

Art of Hopping Tables by Mark Leveridge

And The King of all Restaurant books is Jim Sisti's The Magic Menu

Military Bases, Government Facilities

On military bases and other government facilities you have to show proof of auto and health insurance. Don't play around with the guard at the gate. In most cases your name will be at the gate and Homeland Security has already checked you out. If your work is on a military base you usually will need to furnish your name, last four numbers of your social security, the identification of your vehicle that you will be driving the day of the gig, the reason you are on base, and your contact person.

Therefore, they know who you are when you arrive and you will not get held up at the gate which could make you late for your gig. Frequently screening is required as at an airport. Any items that could be considered a weapon are not allowed. Be aware of any security events which may affect your booking.

Convention Centers/Special Events

If you are working a convention center there are many people that will help you find your way. There is also a map showing the location of all the exhibit halls, meeting, and ballrooms. It is best to arrive early to a convention center that you have never been to since it's easy to get lost You can also go on line to get a foot print/layout of the convention center. Some are bigger than football fields. I have done many trade shows at large convention centers and sometimes it may take 20 minutes to go from the booth you are working to a restroom. See Terminology section on trade shows for additional details.

Trade Shows

Trade shows pay well but are really hard work. I would arrive one day early, check into my room, register at the convention, get my badge, and check out the trade show booth. I would walk around a few times to make sure where our booth is located, not always easy with 500 to 2000 booths. They are numbered but it is easy to lose your way.

Working 8 hours a day at a four day trade show entertaining every 15-20 minutes for the XYZ Company and trying to attract a crowd is not very easy since most booths also have entertainment.

My job is to capture the attention of prospective customers and entertain them with a product message. You are doing a sales pitch for the company's products you are representing at the booth. I worked for a company that wanted me to use some of their buzz words to describe their connector product. I did the classic linking rings as I talked about being connected, giving each ring the name of one of their products. I would do 6 routines 4 times an hour. About the 3d day your ankles and feet start to hurt as you stand on a cement floor all day. I made it a habit of bringing a small rug that I put on the floor behind my table and it gave a lot of relief. I also wore loose fitting socks and brought some Epsom Salt to soak my feet in when I got back to my room. (This advice came from my mother). But even with the small carpet square, walking to and from the break area, restroom, and checking out what other companies were doing is very tiring.

All forms of entertainment can be found at trade show booths, anything to draw a crowd. I've had Hawaiian dancers in the booth to my right and beautiful models in the booth to my left and I'm stopping the crowd with my magic show. After the trade show had closed for the night I may be out with my clients having dinner or at their hospitality room entertaining their prospective customers.

These are a few things you can expect when entertaining at trade shows.

Hospitals and Healthcare Facilities

Entertaining in hospitals is very challenging. I was a volunteer that entertained for elderly patients. At times they would put everyone in a room and I would walk around and entertain them one on one. I found this was better than doing a show on a stage. Once in a while a harpist or a guitarist would come and play some music.

When I was in my teens my mother had a great idea. I did a magic show on a hospital closed circuit TV station. At the end of the 15 minute teaser magic show I stated my name and phone number in case someone wanted to hire me for their party.

Sometimes entertainers at a hospital have to know CPR. During some hospital visits you may be required to have a tuberculosis test and/or flu shot. Do not entertain anywhere if you have a health condition such as a productive cough or open sores which may place others at risk. Protect yourself and others by washing your hands before and after entertaining. Follow the advice of caregivers. Understand the action needed when emergency announcements are made on the intercom.

Sporting Events/Distractions

Being hired at a sporting event may be different. I've been hired for Super Bowl parties at people's homes, local restaurants, The Del Mar Race track on opening day, and working the VIP boxes at Qualcomm Stadium and Petco Park. Here's the problem. Your audience is just not watching you but also the sporting events. Balance your timing so as not to distract the audience from the events they came for.

At times you may be asked to entertain children while the parents are observing the main event. Another time I was entertaining on a sponsor boat during the America's Cup at sea. This was a tough one as guests were trying to watch the race, getting seasick, eating, and drinking. As the boat was bouncing around I was trying to get them to watch me doing magic for 3 hours.

Another time I was hired to entertain a group of students from China on a bus that was taking them from one college to another. The bus was moving and they spoke very little English. You find yourself doing mostly tricks that don't require a lot of talking. This is why magic is a universal form of entertainment.

Special Needs

Entertaining children with special needs such as autism or mental retardation is very rewarding. I entertain for several organizations and hospitals in my city and for children and adults that have challenges. I believe it is important to give back to your community and I do not charge for these performances.

I also have taught magic for children that have disabilities. If you are doing a magic show and there are children with disabilities, never do any tricks that make them look bad, I will do things that make me look silly instead. I will only involve them in a positive way.

Hospitality Suites

Think of this area as a reception for clients and guests. The hospitality suite can have one or more types of entertainers depending on the size of the event.

Whenever I did a trade show my client would host a hospitality suite the previous night for his customers and I would be performing some light magic as the entertainment. Usually people are coming and going and are not dancing. They are just standing around in small groups talking and sharing. There may be a few small tables and chairs for guest as well. If you attempt to offer your services for the trade show and fail, try asking if there will be a banquet dinner or hospitality suite during the convention where you might entertain.

When I'm hired to do one of these rooms there is usually some form of musical entertainment. It could be a classical guitarist, a Jazz duo or even a D.J. playing light background music as well as making announcements. This is an area where a sponsor of the trade show or convention may have a light reception for his clients or customers to show his appreciation. It's in a smaller banquet room and usually they serve finger food, cocktails, and non alcoholic beverages.

Fairs

So you want to work at the county fair? How are you going to break into the fair circuit? You may want to just attend a fair to see how they set up the acts and the exhibits. This is hard work. Although the pay is very good you may do 3 to 6 shows a day, seven days a week for 3 to 6 weeks. If you ever wanted to find out where the cotton candy and stuffed animals come from not to mention the racing pigs and tractor pulls for a specific fair then attend a fair association convention.

The best way is to join a fair association in your area. In the west coast we have the WFA Western Fair Association, WE International Fair Expedition, OFA Oregon Fair Association, and AFA Arizona Fair Association.

The first year you will want to go as a non vender and get a feel for how the fair is run and learn a few things Big fairs are held at various times of the year and many are held in the fall.

The great thing about attending one of these fairs is that you will get a Membership Directory describing where all the fairs are located and the operating dates. You will also obtain information such as who's in charge of the entertainment, fair attendance, and what percentage are adults and children.

Voice-over

If you have a knack for doing different voices, this may be for you and you will work in a variety of settings. I have a friend of mine in San Diego that was very successful as a party D.J. One day he went to a voice-over audition. Now he's doing over 25 commercials a year for radio and television.

I have a deep voice and people have told me that I would be a great radio announcer or voice over artist. I did a few jobs but I have not had any professional training and did not pursue the art. A voice over artist does off camera or off stage commentary.

Hard to Work Events

Reunions of any sort, including high schools, colleges, and families.

High school, college, and family reunions are very difficult to entertain since most people have not seen each other in a very long time and it's hard to hold their attention.

Then there are events that may have a strong emotional impact such as entertaining children with life threatening diseases, for instance-"Make a Wish". I do these but it is difficult.

Chapter 4

PREPARING FOR YOUR GIG

Be on Time

I set my clock 5 minutes fast in my bathroom and in my car. You want to get a bad reputation? Arrive late at a gig. No one wants to hear any lame excuses about being stuck in traffic or your GPS wasn't working.

It's better to arrive 30 minutes early and read a book or set your props with no stress than it is to be sitting in traffic stressing out whether or not you will arrive on time or not.

ALWAYS give yourself plenty of time to get to the event.

Gas

Always make sure you have enough gas in your vehicle before you leave for your gig. You don't want to stop for gas on the way to your job for 2 reasons: 1. It could make you late and 2. You will smell like gas

Check List

Different types of gigs require various types of dress and equipment. Be prepared. Forgetting an important item may ruin your performance. Make a detailed check list of everything you will need, even the obvious items. If you need to change your outfit at the location you may have forgotten to bring the cowboy hat that goes with western costume.

One time I forgot the rabbit. I know a flute player that arrived at a gig without his flute! I've seen a balloon twister arrive without his pump. He had to blow up every balloon by mouth.

The check list can be on paper, a smart phone, computer, or any convenient system that works for you.

Emergencies

Be prepared for emergencies especially if you are in a new location. Know the location of all exits and how to quickly call for help, fire, or other emergencies. Then there are emergencies related to your equipment or your own performance.

Early in my career I met a famous actor named Buddy Hacket who gave me some sound advice which was "always carry a spare fuse". In those days much our equipment had certain fuses, bulbs, and other special items. You may not be able to perform your act unless you can substitute failed parts. Literally, having that spare fuse may save your performance. Even with the latest high technological equipment it is important to have a thorough understanding of what to do if it fails. What will you do if the lights go out, your sound fails, or your guitar string breaks?

Flexibility

An entertainer needs to be ready for a variety of situations and attire. He may need to wear beach attire, roaring 20's, cowboy, pirate, gangster, riverboat, and Mexican Fiesta outfits. You will look out of place if you show up in a tux at a western or a pirate party. These events always need music and some putty (smaller novelty) type entertainment for the cocktail hour such as magicians, palm readers, or caricature artists as an icebreaker.

I was at a hotel one night and in addition to my walk-around sleight-of-hand, there was a 3 piece jazz band and two caricature artist doing funny pictures for some bankers at a convention. The next night I was out on the bay for one of the harbor excursions working for some attorneys that were part of The Bar Association. Be prepared to enjoy unique settings.

Entertainers work at a variety of locations and need to be flexible.

There are large destination companies that plan corporate events. One time five magicians were hired to entertain on buses that were transporting the guests from their hotel down town to a park 30 miles away. It was difficult to entertain on a moving bus. Another time the client had us entertainers hide in the restroom until the bus was in motion and pop out and entertain like magic.

I was hired once to entertain on a bus full of 13 year olds that were on their way to Disneyland from San Diego. A friend followed me all the way to Disneyland. After the client paid me, my friend drove me back to San Diego. The life of the entertainer is never dull

Directions

It is extremely important to be on time for your gig.

I have a reputation with clients that I'm always a minimum of 30 minutes early before show time. This puts everybody at ease. One time I arrived 30 minutes early but when I met the client at the convention center, we had a 20 minute walk to where the party was taking place. I had about 10 minutes to catch my breath and get ready to perform.

The most important consideration is to have accurate directions and be aware of possible causes for delay. Even though the subject of directions is partially covered in other sections of this book it is worth to consider some reminders such as:

When booking a gig get detailed directions.

When available, ask the client to send you a copy of the invitation sent to the guests as it usually includes directions.

Use your global positioning system (GPS) when available.

Use the internet and other technologies like Google, MapQuest, or Rand McNally for maps/directions.

AAA members can use their services to obtain printed Directions and alerts about possible delays.

Local radio stations periodically provide traffic information.

Do not depend on one source for directions, names of streets may change, new streets and addresses may not be listed.

Have paper maps as backup if other systems fail. There are specialty maps such as Thomas Bros. Guide in California.

Consider the time needed when booking more than one event on the same day.

Leave extra time for delays which could occur due to traffic jams, costume changes, accidents, restroom, eating, mistakes, etc.

When possible always know more than one way to reach your destination and don't be afraid to ask for directions.

Have your client's telephone number readily available to call or text if needed...

Keep records of your mileage for billing and tax purposes.

Reliable Transportation

Don't rely on friends or relatives to take you to a gig that you booked two weeks ago. Always call a few days ahead to confirm transportation to your gig.

Reliable transportation is key to be a successful entertainer.

If you have your own vehicle make sure the day before that you have gas and it is running properly. As I have stated previously in this book, being on time is critical to your success. Being delayed in traffic is not a good reason to be late. If something unexpected delay occurs, call your client as soon as possible and then the tow truck or whatever service is needed.

Once you get a reputation for arriving late, agents and event planners won't call for your services.

One time when I was four blocks from my gig I had a flat tire. I called a cab and arrived just in the nick of time. Another time I broke a radiator hose about 2 miles from the hotel, I pulled over to the side of the road and started walking 10 blocks to the hotel. Fortunately a band member happened to see me and picked me up. Never hitchhike as it is too great a risk.

Parking

Know the area where you are to perform.

Parking can be a problem, especially down town. I carry a zip lock bag of quarters, nickels and dimes in my glove box. (If the car next to yours has its red flag up, be nice and drop a quarter in so they don't get a ticket!) You could leave your card in his meter.

Some parking garages will give you a monthly deal. But If I started at 6 PM I would try to find a metered parking spot around 5:30 and feed the meter for 30 minutes since parking was free at the meters after 6 PM. Big garages can be very expensive. I also have commercial plates and after 6 pm I can park in the yellow zones. White zones are for loading and unloading. If you park there you will get a ticket. Never park in handicapped parking, it could cost hundreds of dollars.

Red zones are off limits as well. Some towns have big lots with spaces that have a number for every space. There is a box on the corner of the lot with numbered slots and you put money in the slot with your number. Always carry a few ones, fives and ten's as well as lots of quarters. Some of these lots take your debit or credit card, but to be safe make a note in your date book of when you were in that lot and how much you paid for how long.

Always ask for a receipt, attach it to your booking sheet, and remember it's a tax write off.

Unusual Parking Problems

We all have those places that we hate to work because the parking is bad. When I have a party near the beach I request a parking spot in their driveway. If it's a public place and I know that a lot of walking is going to be involved, I always charge $10.00 to $20.00 more as I may have to pay for parking in a lot or have a Pedi cab drive me to the event. (Pedi cabs are guys on bicycles that have a little couch on the back, figure $1.00 per block).

In San Diego bad parking problems are down town, Balboa Park, and the beach. One time I walked 10 blocks to get to a retirement party. (On a hot Saturday afternoon in my black Zoot suit with leather wing tip shoes with my magic case under one arm and my folding table under the other arm). I usually have one case and a table stand (restaurant tray jack is perfect). Never again. I arrived 15 minutes before show time. Not only was I exhausted but hot and sweaty.

I checked in with the client and tested the microphone. I set up my show, dashed to the restroom to wash my face with cold water, folded up a paper towel and put it in the headband of my hat and walked out just as the M.C. was introducing me. As I was walking towards the stage I was praying for strength to do my show and entertain these people. As it turned out, the show went great and no one knew my pain. I was lucky to catch a cab back to my truck where I collapsed and took a 3 hour nap.

Always give yourself plenty of time in case the parking is terrible. Make a list of all the places that have bad parking and where the alternate parking options are. No city is going to publish a list of "bad parking areas" You will have to find them the hard way.

Safety

If you are alone walking back to your car, be aware of your surroundings. Entertainers (mostly musicians) are usually the first to arrive and the last to leave the events. Your hands are usually full. Always park in a well lighted area. If it's late at night, walk with another person if possible. Carry a loud metal whistle on your key chain.

Transporting Necessary Entertainment Materials

Especially during times of high security you may have difficulty in transporting certain needed materials on airplanes or other means of transportation. Be prepared for that eventuality. You may be able to purchase these items near your gig. If you have large expensive objects such as musical instruments, renting is an option. Always ask the airline what is permissible to bring in your carry on and checked baggage.

Remember that checked bags can get lost or sent to another destination. Therefore do not check any materials you must have for your gig. One option is to ship the material in advance to a responsible person in the area. Another idea for D.J.s is to have the music that is needed on your laptop in case your CD's are lost.

One time Joe Mystic and I had a two day show in Palm Springs. We were hired to do two shows for the same client at her home. We were doing a big illusion that included rabbits and doves. We also had female assistants. It was too expensive to get a hotel room and too far to drive back and forth to San Diego, so we rented a motor home and passed the cost on to the client as travel expenses. It worked out really well as we hooked up a trailer to the motor home that carried all of our magic, costumes and sound equipment.

Equipment Loading/Unloading

It is not good practice to move your equipment through the lobby of a hotel or other establishment especially like the Ritz. It could be an embarrassment and you may be asked to leave. Also persons in the area could be injured.

Always enter through the loading docks and vender areas if you have anything that needs to be moved in or out. It is best to call the hotel and ask what the best way is to get equipment to the location. Entertainers should always enter through back and side doors.

Stuff I Carry in my Vehicle

As a professional full time entertainer it has taken me many years to determine what emergencies supplies to carry in my vehicle. Having available that one item you may need can make a major difference. You will have to determine what items are to be included for your specific requirements and will vary from my list.

Here are some of the things I carry:

Dental wax	Mints	Gum
Magicians wax	$10.00 quarters	$20.00
Band aids	Rubber bands	Batteries/chargers
Scotch tape	Blank check	Mouth wash
Tooth brush	Tooth paste	Hand wipes
Floss	Wash cloth	Matches
Business cards	Sewing kit	Thumb tip
Flash light	Shoestrings	Emery board
Pencil & paper	Swiss army knife	Nail clipper
Cologne	Deodorant	Hand cream
Cough drops	Silver dollars (4)	First aid cream
Chap stick	Glasses repair kit	Stamps
Travel scissors	Cream	Glasses cleaner
Dice (2)	Tooth picks	Napkins
Sun block	Instant shoe shine	Condoms
Pins (in a film can)	Plastic trash bags	Breath spray
Energy bar	Bottle of water	Comb/brush
Hand soap	Sanitizer	Lighter
Deck of cards	Spare glasses	Sponge
Shaving gear	Wash cloth	Keys
Umbrella	Maps	Magic props
Toilet paper	Pad	

Specific conditions and medicinal drug items as follows:

Heartburn/indigestion

Headache

Prescription drugs

Allergies

Insect repellant

Anti nausea

Anti diarrheal

Infection- wound care

Sterile wipes and bandages

Prescription drugs

Character Costumes

A character costume may represent a recognizable character such as a mascot of an athletic team or a cartoon image.

Several years ago I was a 7' rabbit by the name of "Bumper" that did close up sleight of hand and stage magic in gloves. I was a complete cover up, not just an open face costume. I wore a rabbit head, a tuxedo with rabbit feet and white gloves. I was Bumper the Baffling Bunny for many years and to date the only costumed character to become a member of Hollywood's Famous Magic Castle.

Also, I need to mention that much of my success as Bumper goes to Donna Stilwell (Mrs. Bumper Bunny). She would drive and wait for me, many times in dark alleys and bad parts of town, getting drinks with long straws, and sometimes acting as a guard for Bumper when working at special events.

Costume characters make great money at theme parks and at national athletic events. My all time favorite was The San Diego Chicken. Google him to see what I mean. High school and college mascots are usually non paying jobs, but what an education.

I always wanted my client to know that I have given thought about what I would wear to their event. When I worked at a 50's type diner I would wear what men wore in the 50's, black jacket, white shirt, black tie, pants, shoes, and hat. When I worked, at a western steak house I wore formal western attire, no gun belt, but a western jacket, nice vest, string tie, a cowboy hat with nice pants, and boots or shoes.

When I worked at a pet store I dressed like a veterinarian, white lab coat, colorful smock and khaki pants. These are just some ideas as how to dress. You want to fit in whether you are a musician or a magician. You don't have to invest a lot of money for your costumes. I get most of what I need at thrift and men's resale stores.

If you are going do a special character such as Santa Claus you may need to contact a manufacturer of Santa Suits such as "Adeles of Hollywood", you may pay a little more, but you will be the best looking Santa in your city.

Costume shops have close out sales once a year which is a good time to pick up supplies that you need for your show business career. I usually call all the costume stores to find out when their sale will take place and then mark my calendar. I usually get make-up, gloves, white spats, and an extra red suite as a backup

During the holidays it's advisable to carry a back up jacket and pants in your vehicle.

Theme Costumes

Many times a client will have a party with a theme or perhaps they may ask you to suggest a theme.

Recently I entertained at a western theme party. I didn't want to wear the full cowboy outfit as most don't have the necessary pockets for a magician. So I wore my regular outfit but added a black cowboy hat.

I have an assortment of hats in my closet for most theme parties. In most cases you can get away with black shoes, black socks, black pants, white shirt, and a black vest.

I also have an assortment of wigs and hats such as pirate, sombrero, yachtsman for boat cruises, beachcomber hat for beach parties, gambler straw hat with floral head band for casinos, cowboy hat for western parties (black, straw or pink), pith helmet for jungle and safari parties, rainbow stove pipe hat for kids parties, stoner shag hat for hippy dippy parties, beer stein hat for Oktoberfest events, Santa hat or reindeer antlers for the holiday parties, red, white and blue stove pipe or patriotic top hat for 4th of July and veterans day events, green St. Pats hat for St Patrick's day, black top hat for News Year Eve, wizard hat, fedora for gangster or roaring 20's, black witches hat if you are female, and a jester hat for Mardi Gras.

Sometimes you don't have to wear the entire costume, just enough to reflect the theme of the party. There are times when you may be required to wear a full costume. I suggest that you start preparing for these events by collecting a variety of costumes. I also have some incredible costumes, pirate, cowboy, gangster, safari, riverboat gambler, just to name a few.

RSVP

When guests are formally invited to a party by invitation such as a wedding reception, or anniversary party the host will send out an invitation card to each guest requesting their response. This is the RSVP request and assists the party planner with important info as knowing how much food and drink to provide.

Sometimes I'm invited to stay for dinner as I would be providing the entertainment and also doing a short 30 minute show as an after dinner treat. I too would receive an invite to the party with an RSVP card attached. I know that I'm contracted to be there. The client knows that I'm going to be there, but the party planner may not know that you're going to be there so respond to the card

Keys

Especially in the beginning you may be excited and forgetful. Yikes. I can't find my keys and I have to walk out the door to my gig. Please, keep a spare set of keys hidden somewhere in your house. I have a house key, and car key. I also have a hide- a- key on my vehicle in case I lock myself out of my vehicle or lose my keys on the job. You can look for your keys when you get home after your performance.

Agenda

Usually meeting planners and agents have an agenda that describes when things happen at a special event.

When at a party I will locate the person that hired me, introduce myself, and ask what's on the agenda besides my act. They may say something like this "Mike, you will do your close up magic out here in the foyer from 6 pm to 6:45, at 5:45 my staff will move the guests into the main ball room and the D.J. will be playing some light music. You can wait a few minutes for the guests to find their seats and then entertain a few tables until the salad comes out and then you're done"

Always ask for a written agenda.

Hecklers

When I was doing stand-up comedy magic, a dear departed friend of mine by the name of Al Knox once told me" Never acknowledge a heckler from the stage, he may be funnier than you!" This is sound advice. Never allow them to get you to lose your cool and say things you might regret.

Hotels/Convention Centers

It is important to have a record of every major hotel and convention center in the area you expect to entertain. In case I'm unable to have access to my digital devices I have written copies of addresses, phone numbers and directions to get there. I also record the mileage for my taxes. I make a note of the driving time it takes. These are aids when I'm typing a contract. I know where I'm going to be and how long it will take to get there.

Working with Celebrities

How exciting. You are booked for a gig which includes a celebrity. Perhaps you are on the same program. You may be hired to do a birthday party for a famous person.

I've worked with quite a few celebrities and it is important to be able to recognize a person and why they are famous. Do your research. They may be movie stars, politicians, artists, or authors.

I once did an art show for a person named Peter Max. When I was as a teenager I had 5 of his black light posters in my bed room. I had no idea what he looked like, so when I arrived I was talking to a man in the art gallery for ten minutes before I was introduced to him by my agent as Peter Max. Boy, did I feel silly.

Another time I was working in Palm Springs for a Golden Globe event and I was told that I would be doing magic before Jenifer Hudson sang. I said "Who's that"? The agent asked if I had seen the movie "Dream Girls" I said no. Just then there was a tap on my shoulder, "Hi, I'm Jenifer Hudson."

Another time I was hired to do a birthday bash for a famous author Mark Victor Hansen who was known for his millions of "Chicken Soup for the Soul" books. I drove to his house and was met by someone in shorts and a Tee shirt telling me where to park my car. This time I had done my research. I had seen his picture and read a couple of his books. I said, "Hi Mark Hansen". So remember, do your research!

If you know there is a famous person in the audience, you can ask their permission to mention their name. This is good publicity for both them and you.

Green Room

This is a room set aside for the performers to relax, change clothes, and catch a bite before show time. Green Rooms are found in theaters, casinos, and hotels. It's a room that is usually near the area where the performers are going to work or perform. It's a break area for the acts.

If there was a magic show at a theater, the magicians would wait in the green room until it was time to perform. If a hotel doesn't have dressing rooms you can usually change in the rest room.

Dress Code

I always ask the client, "What is the dress code?" They may say "business" or "business casual;" or even "cocktail attire". As a rule I always try to be the best dressed person at the party. If the men are in suits I would wear a high end suit or a tuxedo. Later I created a look that I wear at all events. They may not remember my name but they loved and remembered my colorful Zoot suits with the colorful tie, spats on my shoes, and matching fedora hat.

An entertainer has to decide what works for him. Inquire from various sources how proper attire is interpreted. Specialty formal wear shops may offer suggestions as to what is appropriate for different occasions.

Opening and Closing Your Performance

Depending on your type of entertainment you may need to have some opening and closing remarks. Perhaps your boss has appointed you to be in charge of the next meeting and to warm up the audience. In these situations I usually start with some clean lighthearted humor which is not religious, racial, sexual, or political.

The key to a successful joke is to know your audience.

One opener I have used is: "I have read that one out of three people are ugly. Let's take a poll. Everyone look to your right, Now look to your left, If they look OK then you're the one."

There are many books on one- liners, jokes, and more of them on line. You also may want to have some closing remarks. If you look like you're having a great time then your audience will have a great time.

Chapter 5

MARKETING

Business Organizations

Be familiar with the business organizations in your community.

You could spend every day of the week at business breakfast meetings or luncheons.

For organizations such as the Lions Club, Rotary, Optimist, or Chamber of Commerce, It is important to find the right group that can provide the most leads for jobs such as NACE (National Association of Catering Executives) and MPI (Meeting Planners International)

Special Locations and Events

In most cases shopping centers or large malls will hire entertainment for special occasions, when they are busy. For instance" Christmas holiday season usually begins the day after Thanksgiving and extends to December 24th. During this season they hire carolers, Santa Clauses, face painters, balloon twisters dressed as elves, puppet shows with a holiday theme, magicians to entertain in the lines for photos with Santa, and musicians to play holiday music for their customers. You should contact the marketing department of the shopping center and indicate your availability.

Hospitality suites, breakout sessions, trade shows, sales meetings, luncheons, client appreciation dinners and convention award banquets are opportunities for entertainers. Join your local Chamber of Commerce and get a copy of who is coming to your convention center. Offer to do the employee picnic or holiday party in exchange for the list of companies coming to your town. Then call those companies, e-mail, or send them your promotional materials and hope they will hire you for their event.

There is big business in conventions. Some cities may distribute a book to its members with the names and the convention contacts as well as the dates when they will be visiting. The companies which come to town for a big convention always have a few big parties that need entertainment. Usually this is when I get a call from an agent to work for these corporate parties.

In most cases the big parties will have a theme. It's always a good idea to have several of the most used themed costumes in your closet.

Slow Business

How's business? "Slow"

Be ready for this. It will happen. What do you do?

The first thing I do is go through my booking sheets for the last 2-5 years and see if there were any children's birthday parties or special events that I think they would want repeated. I make a list of their names and phone numbers, the last times they used me, how much I charged them, and what was the occasion.

I did a child's 7th birthday and now, after 3 years, I called the parents and asked if could do their child's 10th birthday. It's amazing how many of these repeats I get for kids and adult birthday parties.

I know February and March are usually slow months and I need to tighten my belt and make every show count. This is when I post ads to teach magic. I have a post card that reads "Be the life of the party. Learn to juggle, do comedy or magic from one of San Diego's favorite entertainers." These are printed on 3 x 5 cards with my phone number and website and I also carry them with me. I post these anywhere that has a bulletin board, such as coffee shops, diners, and libraries. I mail them to clients that may want to buy someone a magic lesson as a gift. I call all the local agents to remind them I'm still available. It's slow for them too. In some ways you are luckier than a person with a 9-5 job because you can take time to clean out the desk, prepare for your tax appointment, file those papers, and spend time with your family and friends.

It can be very stressful when business is slow. We have to reinvent ourselves, take all the things we know, and turn them into income. Sometimes I meet with my fellow entertainers for breakfast or lunch and brainstorm on how to make some extra cash.

If you have idle time don't just sit there. Use your imagination. Get up and do something good whether or not you will be paid. Help your church, temple or non- profit organization with their special projects such as helping the homeless, picking up trash, and repair projects. You will gain respect and feel better about yourself.

Cold Calling

Cold calling is calling or visiting customers for the first time. Here is how I "cold call".

Review yellow pages from cities with companies that may have 50 or more employees such as attorneys, small doctors' offices, heating and air conditioning companies, catering companies, and banks. They all have an employee party once and sometimes twice a year to boost morale.

You can also go to small cities in your county and pick up news papers from that area and cold call some of those advertisers.

I've also noticed a lot of plumbing trucks with the same name on them that indicates it may be a larger company. I will call the secretary of that organization and ask who is in charge of the summer picnic or holiday party and determine who the customer's decision maker is. Usually the secretary or office manager is in charge of those events.

I found that cold calling works better than other types of advertising. Cold calling is not easy, it takes patience and you must maintain a happy attitude while you are on the phone as it reflects you and your business.

Direct Mail - TV- Social Media

You may find new customers through a targeted mailing list. There are companies that can provide all types of mailing lists including names, addresses, e-mail, and telephone numbers for a fee. At times these lists were very profitable for me.

But be aware there are pros and cons to purchasing a targeted mailing list. On the negative side many of the customers may have moved or are out of business.

One time I contacted a company to get a list of all the agents, wedding planners, and event planners in California. I made a flyer about Magic Mike Stilwell, San Diego's favorite magician, available for this and that and here's my phone number. I sent over a thousand flyers and got only 4 call backs. Two of those asked what my prices were and another wanted to have more info for their mailing list.

Last year I mailed a holiday postcard looking for more holiday shows. I mailed this letter to over 500 of my past customers. The nice two color layout cost $385.00 which included printing, artwork, and postage. I put the mailing labels and postage on all the post cards. I received six calls which resulted in booking two parties and one child's birthday party for $185.00 and another for a Santa on Christmas Eve for $200.00, a total of $385.00 for all the effort. The poor economy at that time may have been a factor. I mailed the post cards out in September. Some people said it was too early and some said too late. It was a beautiful 2 sided holiday advertisement and took up so much of my time that I didn't get my personal and client holiday cards out until the end of December.

Direct mail is used every day. Its effectiveness is sometimes questionable. If you don't believe me look in your mail box and throw out all that are of no interest to you. I get a rifle magazine every month and I don't own a rifle, I also get a ladies handbag catalog every few months. I have no idea how I got on these lists.

A number of customers have stopped reading "snail mail" and are relying on other forms of technology to obtain information and communicate. Keep up to date of other advertising opportunities such as offered by current technologies including TV, web sites, blogs and other social media. Maintain computer literacy, seek expert advice, and continue your education. Don't let opportunity pass you by.

Finding New Business

If you are going to put business cards on a bulletin board, put five in a bulldog clip and use a heavy duty push pin to hold the clip. If you are posting ads use bright colored paper. Also always carry tacks, pushpins, tape, and small magnets for these bulletin boards.

Here's a great way to create a mailing list and get new business. You will have to make sure that it's OK to post this in retail outlets like ice cream, yogurt stores, and barbershops. (Thank you Joe).

Take a 12" box with a locked top and a slot on top. On the outside, print: "Win a free magic show for your Childs Birthday Party. A drawing will be made the first of every month". Next to the box you place entry cards. The cards have questions: Parents Name, Childs Name, date of birth, phone number, and e mail address.

Each month you pick a name at random and do the birthday. Using the above information, start a mailing list and each month call or do an e-mail blast to see if anyone wants to use your services. On the bottom of the cards I put a P.S. "When I entertain at your child's party I will teach your child a special magic trick" I'm always promoting.

I give credit on the back of my business cards to vendors who have given me great deals such as:

Tuxedos by Night and Day Formal Wear or San Diego Formal

Flowers by Grossmont Florist or Spring Valley Floral

Printing from ABC Printing

I also gave out long stem carnations to the waitress's at the steady restaurants where I work. (Write it off as client promotion)

I never put the times that I worked at restaurants. If the guests call to ask for the times I was there. It emphasizes that I had a following and possibly helped me being there longer then contracted.

Every few years I do research to locate company names that are similar to my name "Magic Mike". Here are a few examples: Magic Auto Body, Magic Carpet Care, Magic Dry Cleaners, Magic Touch Home Care, Magic Window Cleaners, Magic Bin Rental and so on.

I designed a post card that looks like a coupon which offers a 10% discount since they use the word "Magic" in their company name. I also print the following:" Hold on to this coupon. Hire professional Magician Magic Mike Stilwell for your next open house, client appreciation party or your company picnic or holiday party". I add my website address, e-mail address and phone number. I print it on high quality paper and have a 10% discount logo in all 4 corners of the postcard with no expiration date. I had a call a couple of years ago from a client who held on to the card but was no longer in that business and she wanted to know if the discount still applied, and of course my answer was yes!

Billboards

Nothing is better for the ego than seeing a 16' tall picture of yourself as you drive down the street. The Corvette Diner restaurant put up a billboard advertisement to celebrate their 10 year anniversary with a picture of the staff and I was in the middle of the picture. For many months people would tell me that they saw me on the freeway sign.

Another time my alter ego "Bumper" was performing at The College Grove shopping center mall and they had a big billboard on the freeway, "Come see Bumper the Magical Rabbit this Easter!" You can't beat this type of advertising. It doesn't happen very often, so when it does, make sure you get a picture of the billboard. If your client doesn't want a billboard you may consider asking if they would consider sharing the cost with you for a large poster in the front of the establishment.

Table Tents

Table tents are folded cards which may be in a plastic folder and placed on a table. When I worked at Black Angus restaurant they had a table tent on each table with my appearances on one side and the drink specials on the other.

At times I provided the table tents in the beginning with my information on one side and suggested that they place their specials on the other side. Soon the restaurant began paying for them.

Restaurant supply venders have a small plastic holder that is perfect for tent cards. They are inexpensive and I have found that if I supply them, the restaurant would use them.

Yellow Pages

With the exception of small towns the use of yellow pages is not effective for entertainers. Currently the major source for bookings is on the internet such as web sites. Repeat bookings and referrals are also significant sources.

I have cancelled all my yellow page advertizing but I kept the courtesy listing that comes with my phone and is listed as Magicians "Magic Mike Stilwell".

If you decide to advertise in the yellow pages don't make the same mistake I made. I made the mistake to be listed under adult entertainment, thinking I was attracting clients that wanted adult entertainment, not a children's show. I was grouped in with the strippers and massage therapists and escorts under "Adult Entertainment".

Caution: Stay up to date to be sure your entertainment ads are not confused with other unrelated forms or characters which may be published on the media.

Internet/Digital

I cannot emphasize enough in 2013 how important it is for an entertainer to understand the enormous importance of internet /digital marketing. It is not an exaggeration to say that you should study intensely to be knowledgeable in this field. To survive as a successful entertainer you must be knowledgeable.

How? Recognize that technology will continue to change at a rapid rate. You will need to change your way of doing things that were successful in the past.

Change is not easy or comfortable but it is extremely necessary for you to keep abreast with the latest state of the art. Build on your own current computer skills, join a computer club, read books on your subject, enroll in your community college and library classes, hire a tutor, seek help from knowledgeable others such as coworkers, other entertainers, and friends.

Start by identifying the social media sources that are used for marketing such as: Amazon, Linkedin, Facebook, Twitter, Google, etc.

In the past you would send a DVD or a CD to your client and they would watch or listen and decide if they wanted to hire you. Now the client can Google your name, look at your web site, or see if you are on You Tube at www.youtube.com. You Tube is an easy way for the public to see a short clip of your actual performance.

Caution: Be careful of language and of want you say on line as it may be interpreted differently from what you intended. Put a firewall on your computer to avoid attacks by hackers. Learn the basic computer terminology. Don't become addicted to computer/digital communication. Evaluate the time spent and the value of the communication.

You must have an e mail address and a web site for your clients. My e-mail is mikestilwellentertainment@gmail.com. I expect that soon 90% of my bookings will eventually come via response to my e-mail/web site.

My web site is www.magicmikesd.com. It has six video feeds that show me performing little snippets at shows and also some bio info and resume of achievements. As a bonus I have a page that lets the person looking at my site enjoy doing some magic tricks as an interactive part of my website.

On the computer you can enter just about anything you can think of in "You Tube". If you ask for pigs in wheel barrows something will pop up. You Tube is a way to share your video with everyone. It allows you to post short videos for the whole world to view. This is a great way to promote your band or act

for the world to see. It also is a way to teach as well. You can go on You Tube to learn a card trick or how to carve a pumpkin.

Be alert for low cost on line advertising. Currently Craig's List is an on-line classified advertising page that is listed for most major cities in the United States. Under the "Community" heading there are listings for Events, Artist, and Musicians. Under the heading "Gigs" you will find Events, Talent and Crew. When looking for work currently, Craig's List can be a great asset.

Publicity

My favorite publicity stunt was to challenge the guests. The managers would run ads that would say: "Bring in your own deck of playing cards, and if our magician cannot do a card trick with them, then we will buy you a dinner". The guests would bring in decks that were round, miniature, oversized, even in Chinese.

When doing a chartable event I would always announce that I was there due to the compliments of my steady gig such as the Corvette Diner where I was resident magician and goodwill ambassador for many years. People would call to find out what time I was there. It was good publicity for the restaurant and for me. Whatever type of entertainer you are, always plug the place where you work as a steady. It's a win- win for everyone... My yellow page ad had a small line under the ad that read: "Corvette Diner Magician since 1987".

When I worked at Black Angus Steak House, I purchased many western costumes from a place called The H bar R, and I had signed pictures of me in a cowboy outfit saying "Thanks for making me look so Goood" Signed: Magic Mike Stilwell, Black Angus Magician. I had a picture in my 50's attire and a local deli placed my picture with all the other local celebrities of San Diego.

I had my picture taken in a tuxedo that I purchased from Night and Day Formal wear. I copied it to an 8 x 10 which said: "My Magic never looked so good. Thanks for the help" signed: Magic Mike Stilwell - San Diego's favorite Wedding Reception Magician.

Publicity is important, and you should never miss an opportunity to promote yourself or the place where you work. I have had a few jobs from each one of these places. I had my picture with a beautiful boutonniere that A La Mesa Florist provided me. I gave them signed pictures which showed their customers that local talent relies on their services.

Communication

Communication with the "Host" staff of the restaurant

There's nothing more embarrassing when a guest calls the restaurant and asks when the magician is performing and the host person has no idea. In some cases they didn't even know they have a magician. So I made up a small flyer which said

"Magician Magic Mike Stilwell performs close-up strolling table to table magic here at the Corvette Diner restaurant every Tuesday and Wednesday from 6-9:00 PM.

I gave it to the manager to place in an obvious location so that everyone that works at the host desk and other staff members will know. If there is valet parking I also give them a flyer. I want to make sure that everyone knows when I'm performing. This is not an ego thing; it's just communication for the guests that will ask about you. My friends call in from time to time to ask "when is the magician there?" If they don't know I start again with the flyers.

Foot in the Door

Whenever I am looking for a gig I first need to get my "foot in the door. I have had great success with offering to come in any night the manager wants, such as "happy hour" and do one hour for FREE. If they and the guests approve I will request a 6 week trial. It's hard to turn down this offer.

Giveaways

I love give-a-ways, and I give anything that has my name on it such as pens, business cards, gags, even flyers that teach you a few tricks. I put cards in tuxedo stores, coffee shops, laundromats, and college bulletin boards. Post everywhere, I even run free ads on various social media.

How do You Market Yourself

The place where you want to work doesn't know that you want to work there. In fact they don't know that they need you.

I like to hang out in places that I'm interested in. Each time after I did a show I would stop by a place where I would like to work. Sooner or later someone would ask me why I'm dressed up and then I tell them. I also will mention to the manager that what I do would promote good business for their happy hour or Sunday brunch.

I try to find who the decision maker is, because the wait staff, the bartender, and even the manager can love you, but without a firm "YES" from that person you are just spinning your wheels. Find out what the best time is to talk to that person. If it's a restaurant or night club the middle of the afternoon is best, usually after lunch or before dinner.

References/Testimonials

On your promotional material it's always good to have at least 5 great references from people that your new client can contact.

I have references for my kids shows, Bar and Bat Mitzvahs, and corporate and trade shows. Make sure you have permission to give phone numbers or e-mail addresses of your references. When I have one of those really great shows I ask my client "Can I use you as a reference?"

A reference is a statement given by a person you have suggested they contact concerning your past experience. A testimonial is an unsolicited statement about a person and is usually complementary such as:" Bob's magic show kept the children and staff well entertained and it was a really fun show", "Thank You, John Smith, and Camp Director."

I have a trunk full of thank you notes from clients which read something like this: "Our Magician Magic Mike Stilwell magically attracted many people at our Trade Show Booth. Larry Thomas, XYZ Company, Cleveland, Ohio."

Agents Business Cards

Whenever I do a corporate magic show for agents they give me a stack of cards to hand out to those asking for one. (I have said this before, NEVER pass out your card on an agent job).

I have a collection of cards and file them separately under each agent's name. It's a great way to organize agent business cards. Now when I have a job for a specific agent I take a few cards with me so when an agent asks "do you need any of my cards"? I say no and show him I'm prepared. This really makes me look good. I have a small business card size pocket sewed in my jacket just for business cards.

Press Releases

Review the press releases about other entertainers that you have seen on TV, magazines or other forms of communication. Think of a human interest story related to a charity event or perhaps something that is really unusual about your work.

Here is an example of a successful press release when I performed in costume as a magical bunny. When I first created "Bumper the Baffling Bunny" a friend of mine, John Ferguson who worked at a local TV station, was very instrumental getting Bumper off the ground. He wrote a press release and told me to send it to all the TV and radio stations. Because of that release I was hired for some local TV shows, a radio station interview, and I was booked at a local restaurant performing magic. It lasted for 2 years and after it closed I was engaged at another restaurant that lasted for 8 years.

All the release said was: "Seven foot two, eyes are blue, has any one seen the magic that Bumper can do? Keep a watchful eye out for Bumper the Baffling Bunny. A rabbit that does more than pull a magician out of his hat" This was attached to a 5 x7 black and white picture of Bumper. Later I had a couple of TV commercials as Bumper and also as some nice newspaper exposure.

Human Touch

Whenever I'm hired for a special occasion like a birthday, anniversary or holiday party I give the guest of honor a special occasion card with a note that states "I hope I added a touch of my magic to your special day, sincerely, Magic Mike Stilwell"

Recently I was hired to do a memorial, a celebration of life, and I brought a card with me. A few weeks later I received a letter thanking me for the fun entertainment and the nice card. People appreciate that you are more than an entertainer and that you're human as well. I have an accordion file full of hospitality cards for every situation.

Magnetic Signs

Magnetic signs for advertising are relatively inexpensive and easily attached and removed from your vehicle and always remember that if you cut someone off on the freeway they may call you about it.

I purchased magnetic signs for my vehicle and one day at a fund raiser for a church benefit someone stole my signs... Now I take them off and put them on at each event. The signs are great advertizing.

Thank you Cards

I feel it is important to thank clients in person and other means such as: e-mail, text messages, or post cards with the message such as:
"I really appreciate your business",
"Thank you for having me at your party!"
"I hope that we get a chance to do it again soon, Sincerely, Magic Mike Stilwell."

Customer Service

I credit most of my success as a professional entertainer to great customer service. I try very hard to give the client everything they want and more. Many times the client doesn't know exactly what they need or want and rely on me to inform them what is needed for their special event.

For instance, I had a client call me and requested magic at her event. This particular event was her 20th wedding anniversary and she was inviting different types of people and thought my magic would be a great ice breaker. There would be people from her work, church, book club, her husband's work, his poker buddies, and all of their children and families. There would be from 150 to 200 guests at this event. I suggested that I would be a roaming magician doing close-up magic working small groups at a time. When she asked for the cost I quoted $400 for 90 minutes at the cocktail hour and I suggested that she have a classical guitarist or a pianist play after I was gone as background music. She asked "How much for 30 minutes?"

I had made a big mistake because I didn't first ask if she had a budget for entertainment. I assumed that since she was having a large party in a fancy hotel she had sufficient money for entertainment. I explained that if I were there for only 30 minutes some guests would not see my magic and since the guests know a magician will be at the party some will be disappointed to not have seen me perform. This sounded like a great party. I told her I had another event that day and I if she was flexible about the time I could give her a better deal. This is where I get what I need time wise and the client wins too. In this case the client was flexible and I gave her a lower price. She was very satisfied and I didn't need to rush from one gig to another.

So often I see entertainers looking at their watch like they can't wait for the event to be over or their time to be over. I don't even wear a watch. I stay longer on purpose. I always give extra time and I have a reputation of doing that. My past clients tell others "Mike always gives us more than we pay for"

I believe in "Givers Gain" and I would want that on my tomb stone when it's time.

Chapter 6

LAWS/LEGAL ISSUES

Insurance, General Liability

Your situation may be unique but if you are booking your work as an individual or being hired by an agent you must consider legal issues and related polices

When I worked at shopping centers, grad nights, schools or theme parks the contracting agents always wanted proof of Commercial Liability Insurance and possibly health test and health insurance. This coverage can vary and be in the millions. In some situations magicians and jugglers need to have proof that they have a certificate of liability insurance and if they worked for a theme park they have to confirm that the park is additionally insured and protected by their insurance policy.

Sometimes musicians are covered by the agents that booked them or the Musician's Union.

I understand that D.J's need liability insurance to work for clubs and restaurants and that the cost can be several hundred dollars a year. No matter what you do as an entertainer everyone wants to be covered.

The International Brotherhood of Magicians, Society of American Magicians, and The World Clown Association offer a group policy.

Over the years magicians had Hartford, Colony, and Lloyds of London as carriers for their insurance. The producer was Sports and Special Event Risk Purchasing Group Inc.

It's getting difficult to find companies that will protect entertainers such as magicians, hypnotists, clowns, palm readers, stilt walkers, face painters, fire eaters, sword swallowers, acrobats, animal acts, and musicians.

Do research and talk with colleges in your special entertainment field for advice about insurance and liability.

Entertainers Agreement/Contract

In the early stages of being an entertainer your customer may be someone you know such as family or friend. You may decide that a written contract is unnecessary. This could also pertain to a steady gig when you are not represented by an agency. Even though you have only a verbal commitment you should have a booking sheet and send your client a monthly invoice (bill).

When you have been contacted by an agent, talent agency, or producer and you may have a verbal understanding concerning the working arrangements, it is still important to have a dated written agreement signed by you and the client/agent before you begin working.

Although there will be variations of individual needs there are a number of common elements such as: date, names, time, place for the event, method of communicating with key contacts, financial arrangements, liability insurance requirements, policy requiring distributing business cards, responsibility of the entertainer as an independent contractor, policies related to behavior concerning alcohol/drugs/smoking, food availability, and other special instructions.

Remember to check that your agreement/contract corresponds to the notes on your original booking sheet. Also remember that since this is a legal contract you are responsible to carry out your part of the agreement.

Should you have any questions it is advisable to seek an attorney's advice.

Health Insurance

Some theme parks require that you must have liability insurance and also health and vehicle insurance. You may have a full time job that provides your health insurance or your spouse or parents may have you on their plan.

When you are self employed you have to provide your own insurance. You may search for "Health Insurance for Self Employed" in your state.

Starting in 2013 under the Obama Affordable Health Care Act entertainers must study and find out how these new requirements and significant changes will affect their benefits and health insurance cost.

Income Tax

Starting immediately as an entertainer you must keep accurate records for filing income tax returns. Use the internet or visit your local Internal Revenue Service (IRS) office to obtain instructions. If necessary consult a Certified Public Accountant (CPA). Also obtain advice from your colleges and professional organizations.

Some of the records you will need for the IRS are:

Miles travelled for each gig, parking, business miles, vehicle expenses, income including tips, Internet/mobile phones, data usage, office expenses, costumes, cleaning, insurance, business meals, lodging, equipment props, advertising, postage, association dues, trade show expenses, value of charity events, continued education in your field, and other expenses.

Don't get into the habit of accepting payment for your services and not recording it as income for tax purposes.

Chapter 7

ETHICS/BEHAVIOR

Attendance

You have finally obtained a steady job. This is called your "STEADY". You are employed for specific days at certain hours. At times you may need to have another entertainer substitute (sub) for you.

If you want to create a following, DON'T sub yourself for a higher paying job. The place where you are working as a stead takes care of you each month, week, and day. Should you sub yourself out, two bad things happen: The first is that management sees a different person than the one he hired, and may not be what they expected. Or the person may be much better than you, and guess what; you could be replaced by your sub. The next thing is that some of the guests expect to see you every week and are disappointed that you are not there. Also they may have brought in someone special to see you which compounds the problem for everyone. Sometimes the entertainer is not there because his wife is having a baby or because he was sick. This is understandable.

It is UNACCEPTABLE if the entertainer does not appear because he got a higher paying gig and sent someone in his place. The restaurant or club pays you when business is slow or busy. Your steady is exactly that, a "STEADY".

In my 15 years at a local diner I missed only 12 days and in my 8 years at another restaurant I missed 8 days. I may have lost about 30 gigs by not taking them the nights I was committed to my "Steady" but I stayed with the steady gig. Even my vacations were around my schedule.

If you want to create a following you have to be there when guests come back. I've seen many entertainers sub themselves out of a job. Also, No Call, No Show, or No Fill in for a night when people are expecting entertainment, is reason for termination. In addition your reputation will be damaged as an entertainer.

Sick

If you have a day job you can call in sick and no one really cares. "Ok, see you when you feel better"

Ever hear the expression, "The show must go on!" This concerns most single acts like comics, magicians, hypnotists, disc jockeys, ventriloquist, actors, and master of ceremonies. If you play a musical instrument in a band or orchestra or even with a singer, you may be able to get a replacement since it probably won't change the continuity of the music and no one will notice unless you are the headliner.

If you have a broken leg or are on your death bed you will probably not do the show. The folks that aren't in show business will not understand. "Why not call the client and tell them that you are sick"? I'm not recommending you work under extreme conditions such as when you're contagious or bleeding severely. You will understand after you have spent a few years as an entertainer. It's your passion. You just don't call in sick for minor problems.

You have been booked months and perhaps years in advance. There has been an agreement with the client, a reservation fee has been paid to you, the client and guests are expecting you.

Most professional entertainers will tell you exactly how many shows they have missed during their career. They may have established a relationship with a fellow entertainer who will substitute when needed in a serious emergency. I've missed 12 shows in my 40 years as an entertainer because I was too sick to perform. It doesn't happen often. You just don't call your client and say "Hi, I won't be making it tonight, I don't feel well". It's not an option.

Language

Avoid expressions and language that could be offensive to your audiences. This includes sex, bathroom, race, occupation, physical handicaps, ethnicity, politics, religion etc.

Dating/Sexual Harassment

Dating people where you are working is a no-no. As some sayings go "Never dip your pen in the company inkwell", "Don't fish at the company pier" and many others that boil down to, do not date anyone where you work. Don't respond to familiar approaches by customers or work force personnel.

Sexual harassment is a very important item to consider in the entertainment field. It seems the opposite sex likes to flirt with entertainers and some do it even while with their partners.

Be very careful. We are different from people associating with their peers at work or people they associate with on a day to day basis. Be cautious, the person that is flirting with you might be the client's mate. Because someone is being nice to you doesn't mean that they want anything more from you than your job as an entertainer. Don't confuse being nice to you is flirting with you.

Remember, you are there to entertain, not dating. I had this problem as a trade show performer where the audience was away from home and wanted to have some fun. Be very careful of what you say and how you say it. You don't want to be misunderstood. If you sense that you were misunderstood clear it up immediately or apologize for the misunderstanding. This is not just for the audience, but also for entertainers.

I once said to a female singer whom I really admire as an entertainer. "Are you and the lead guitar player co-habituating?" I was trying to be funny since they were kidding each other. Later she took me off to the side and told me in no uncertain terms that she didn't appreciate that I intruded in her conversation and making a rude comment. I offered my sincere apology and it helped relieve any tension. I worked with this act for the next few months and we had a good relationship.

I know entertainers that try to date while they are working but some day they may find they do not have a job. They also get a bad reputation and that's bad especially with agents.

I took a date to see an act one time and after we were seated I excused myself and went to the rest room. While I was gone the entertainer we came to see was hitting on my date (She told me later). When I approached the table he quickly changed his tune to "Hi Mike what's new?"

Sexual Harassment is common in every type of work area. We are NOT exempt just because we are entertainers. One time a lady walked up to me while I was performing and said, "I'll bet he's really good with his hands" as she winked to all the ladies around me. I did not acknowledge the statement. I just kept doing what I do. Entertain.

Sexual harassment is not just touching. It can also be other types of inappropriate behavior such as comments about the body, jokes in bad taste, verbal statements that are obvious that you're making some kind of sexual advancement, and talking about sex makes people uncomfortable.

Remember you are on a job to entertain, just do that; don't hit on the opposite sex, be over flirtatious, touch anyone other than shaking hands, and only hug people that you are sure they want to be hugged. Make it quick so no one feels uncomfortable. Do not say things that could be taken the wrong way. You are hired to entertain.

Children

When entertaining children make sure that adults are present.. Be aware at all times of behavior that may be misunderstood and be current about sexual harassment laws.

Alcohol

Don't ever drink on the job, even if the client insists. PASS! Don't even drink the day before your job. The odor of alcohol can be detected by others.

Drugs/Medication

Be aware that all drugs including prescription medications can affect your behavior. Know how each drug will affect you.

Chapter 8

ETIQUETTE AND APPEARANCE

Appearance

You must take pride in the way you look, speak, smell, and your general appearance. Be professional.

I have seen entertainers that look like they just rolled out of bed, had bad breath, and body odor. You should not show up at work with grease under your fingernails or paint on your hands, or even worse, bad body odor. YUCK! Even spectators viewing a street entertainer are offended.

Also, when not entertaining, people may recognize you so be aware of your appearance and demeanor.

Keep smiling and project a happy attitude.

Personal Grooming Reminders

These "Reminders" may seem like common sense,
　　But:
　　Always brush your teeth after a meal.
　　Rinse your mouth with a mouth wash just before show time.
　　Don't overdo after shave lotion or perfume.

Use under arm deodorant.
Take a bath/shower daily or more often if necessary.
Always be sure to wash your hands and clean nails before show time.
If you have dandruff, seek treatment or don't wear a black shirt or jacket.
Give yourself plenty of time to put on your makeup.
Don't drink alcohol the day of or the night before your performance.
Don't drink or eat foods that cause heart burn, bad breath, or gas.
Keep a supply of clean tissues/handkerchiefs.

Chapter 9

CONTINUED GROWTH IN YOUR SKILL

Practice Practice Practice

A wonderful magician and entertainer, Mr. Magic aka Mr. Bill Smith told me, to be successful in anything that you want to do you must remember these three things. Practice, Practice, and when you're done Practice again. I never forgot those three words, and I pass them along to you and everyone I have ever taught.

Your entertainment would be considered a hobby if you only want to tie balloon animals occasionally, play the flute when guests come over, do magic just for your friends or the school talent show. Perhaps you don't have to work as hard as a professional.

If you want to be a professional entertainer you must practice your craft diligently and perform at every opportunity. Go to a park in your neighborhood and practice. I used to practice for the people at a bus stop and subway platform. Some of my friends still don't want to see my card tricks because they were tired of my saying, "You want to see a card trick?" Regardless, you still need to keep practicing.

Clubs / Organizations /Trade Magazines

There are clubs for all types of entertainers such as clown clubs, comic clubs, etc. If your specialty is not listed in the next section look in the internet or research other sources.

For example, as a magician I can locate a magic club in every major city in the world. As of 2012 I have been a member of the local International Brotherhood of Magicians since 1976, The Society of American Magicians since 1974, and Hollywood's Prestigious Magic Castle since 1981. I can share some thoughts and get advice from my peers.

The most important thing about being part of a club with people that love the same thing you do is the fellowship and opportunity to brainstorm new material. These clubs usually meet once a month, and if you are traveling they will treat you as a welcomed guest.

Trade Clubs and Magazines

Magician
The oldest magic club is "The Society of American Magicians" (SAM)
Its magazine is MUM (Magic, Unity, Might)
The "International Brotherhood of Magicians" Club (IBM)
Its magazine is The Linking Ring
The Magic Castle and the Academy of Magical Arts
Genii, The International Conjuror's Magazine
The Magic Circle: The club is in London
Magic Magazine: An independent magazine for magicians

Jugglers
"International Jugglers Association" (LJA)
Jugglers World is their magazine
"Kaskade" a European Juggling Magazine
"The Catch" a U.K. Juggling Magazine

Caricature Artist
"International Society of Caricature Artist" (ISCA) The magazine is called "Exaggerated Features"

Clowns
"World Clown Association" (WCA) "Clowning Around" is the magazine

Santa Claus
The international club is called "FORBS) "Federation of Real Beard Santa's"

Musicians
Musicians Association,
If you are a professional musician you probably will join your Musicians Union or Association. San Diego is Local 325

Balloon Twisters
"Balloon Magic" the magazine
This magazine is published by one of the largest balloon manufactures "Quaiatex".
Also, the World Clown association can help.

Face Painting
Here are 3 magazines
"Face Painting""Face to Face" and Ameridan face painting Magazine.
World Clown Association is a good resource.

Hypnotist
The Hypnotist Magazine
Hypnosis Monthly

Psychic
Including Palm readers, tarot card readers, tea leaves
Psychic Reader Magazine
Prediction Magazine
New Vision Psychic Magazine

Ventriloquist
Oracle Ventriloquist Magazine
  Ventriloquist Journal

TV/Radio
To do commercials on TV and radio you need to be a member of "AFTRA"
  American Federation of TV and Radio and "SAG" Screen Actors Guild.

Colleagues

I try to meet with colleagues that are in my occupation at least 4 times a year even though they are competitors. Once every couple of months a few magicians meet to have breakfast and discuss everything from new tricks to clients that don't pay for our routines and even personal things about our families. Occasionally when a person that is well known in our industry comes to town we meet and take this person to lunch or dinner. This can be a lot of fun!

Watch other Entertainers

In the beginning and in addition to watching many live entertainers I listened to comedy records over and over to hear their timing on jokes and stories. I listened to cassettes, CD's and watched VHS/DVD videos of magicians and comics to see how they performed on stage. Now we can watch a multitude of entertainers on computer sites such as You Tube.

DON'T STEAL ANOTHER ENTERTAINERS BITS, ROUTINES, OR LINES. IT'S NOT ETHICAL AND MAY BE ILLEGAL.

Watch, learn, and listen how other entertainers control the audience, watch how they tell a joke or a funny story that sounds real, look at how they are dressed, how they engage the audience and how they treat volunteers on stage. Find someone you really admire and watch his presentations, his patter, and how and when the audience reacts. Watch and learn, take notes, make a record of what you want to remember.

Starting a Business

You have progressed in your entertainment skills from hobbyist to part time and now full time employment as an entertainer. You have established your entertainers name and will be "Doing Business As" (DBA) with that name.

You may want to start a small entertainment business. This requires effort, skill, education, and time. Take classes related to small business and seek assistance from your local colleagues and business organizations. You will probably have additional needs for space, equipment, and supplies.

Know the state and local laws related to starting your business such as: business license, registration with appropriate agencies, publishing your business name and location, bank accounts, and IRS requirements.

Funding may be available for special groups such as: veterans, women's, minorities, etc. Much information can be found on the internet and libraries.

You can now market your talents to: radio stations, catering companies, casinos, event planners, talent agents, advertising agents, wedding planners, amusement parks, zoos, destination companies, resorts, hotels, and food and beverage managers. What do all these type of companies have in common? They all need entertainment with entertainers.

Other Entertainers

You can expect to work with a wide variety of special entertainers in your area who have skills different from yours. Get acquainted with them as you can learn a lot from each other.

Most of these entertainers are professional and this is what they do for a living. Check them out on the internet.

In addition to those that I have mentioned previously here are some of the other entertainers that I've worked with in San Diego (In no particular order):

Santa: Loren Smith (He was my "Santa" mentor) Real Bearded Santa

Other real bearded Santa's are Joe Mystic and Larry Frankel
Body Art: Betty Lovegen (She also does Mrs. Claus as well) & Star Shields

Carolers: Janet Hammer Street Entertainers: "Sleeveless", Jim Hershey

Stage Magicians: Joe Mystic & Terry Lunceford & Monty Stratton

Puzzle Master: Harry Eng Gambling Expert: Richard "The Cheat" Turner

Close-up Magicians: My Mentor J.C. Wagner, Curtis Clark, Godfrey, Stephen "Sleeveless" Sloan, Owner of The Gathering Restaurant, Dan Thomas, Sebastian Figueroa owner of The Red Spade Magic Theater, Craig Stone, Jeff Martin, Tom Ogden Comedy Magician of the year for more years than anyone else at The Magic Castle, Jeff Marcus, Derrick "The Persian Prince", Chuck Martenez, Brad Burt, Gary Vess, and James Kellogg owner of The local Magic Shops.

Face Painter Balloon Twister (Author or 5 balloon books) stilt walker and magician: Jon "Dooney" Johnson

Jugglers: Brad French, Larry Keough, David Kamatoy, Kit Summers, The late Randy Foster (this guy made me laugh so hard, he would crack me up on gigs we shared together,

Silhouette Cutter: Randy Parish Bell. By the way there are only a few people who do this type of work. It's an art form all in its own.
Unicyclist: Tim Kern

Singing telegrams, commercial artist, character actor, balloon twister, and all around fun guy: Steve Chavez

Mimes: Larry ": Star" Keough and Jerry "Kazoo" Hager

Clowns: DeeGee the Clown, Melody Childers,
Jeff "Senator Sandwich" Marcus

Stilt Theater: Liii Noden

Puppet show: Gil and Laurie Olin

Acrobatic shows: Pete and Rachell Wray

Mentalist: Max Maven and David Winston

Xylophone or marimba: Carl Mack

Caricature artist: Court Jones, Diane Atteberry, and John Wismont

Percussionist: Warren Bryant

African Musician: Akai Akayaa

Sax, flute, wind instruments: Adrienne Nims

Mariachi's: Pedro Gonzalez "Mariachi Real"

Balloon twister that does the entire cartoon characters which are at least 2 to 4 feet tall: Dave Gonsalves (He can be found sitting next to face painter Betty Lovegren at Seaport Village in Down Town San Diego.) He's been there for over 25 years as a balloon twister vender.

Solo male singer: Mr. Bernie Kaye. I once heard him sing "The Lords Prayer" a cappella in the key of C at a funeral, for Mr. Jim Deacy. It was beautiful.

Bemie was a band leader and drummer for over 50 years as well as an entertainment producer and agent in San Diego. First with "The

Music People" and "Entertainment Solutions West, Inc." My mentor in the Entertainment Producer Business.

Students of mine in magic that became professionals: Sebastian Fegueroa, Diane Lane and Victor Ballesteros.

Classical guitarist: Eric Foster. Chinese Zither: Cathy Li

Accordionist: Al Jacobs Pick Pocket: Apollo Robbins

Dove worker magician: Marshal Silver & "Great Scott" Farr

Names on rice and wax hands: Carin Alexander

Palm and tarot card reader: Carole Nance

Write and sing children's music shows: Larry Keogh and "Campfire" Kath Eckert

Magician bartenders: Bob Sheets, J.C. Wagner, Terry Lunceford, Joe Mystic,

Trade show magician who taught me the trade show business: Mike Rogers

Fairs and festivals: Terry "Godfrey" Godfrey, Nick Sharpe and Jeff Martin

Hypnotist: James Kellogg Jr., Joe Mystic, Paul Le Blanc, Jeff Marcus, Marsha Star, Barry Jones

Disc Jockeys "D.J.'s" Ed Bia, Eric Sands, Greg Rackley, Robert John D.J and karaoke, Russ McKamey

Children's magic shows: Joe Mystic, Rich Roberson, Michael Johnson "Amazing Dana" Law, John Johnson.

Line dance instructor and dance school: Liz O'Grady

Stand up Comics: Frank King, Kurt Swan, Chris "Zooman" Klauber & Diane Jean

The Bubble Man: Keith Walters

Celebrity Look a Likes: Glenn Ford- John Ferguson, Marilyn- Bethany Owen, Elvis-Matt Way, Ed Sullivan and Groucho-Jerry Hoban, Austin Powers-Richard Halpern

Voice -over Artist for radio and T.V. Commercials: "Shot Gun" Tom Kelley

Chapter 10

YOUR HEALTH

Rest

Often I arrive at events 20-40 minutes early. This happens if the traffic is normal, it was easy to find a parking spot, or I was running really early. I tend to take a little shut eye and I set the alarm for 15-20 minutes and relax. If you are a heavy sleeper or are really tired, DON'T do this. However I'm always refreshed after I do. I have a cooking timer in my glove box that I can set for hours and minutes. Mine rings a bell for 10 seconds but there are some that buzz. Often I have 60-90 minutes between shows, not enough time to run home, but enough time to catch a nice relaxing snooze as I'm waiting for the next gig.

Trade Show Stress on Families

Trade shows are hard on families and on marriage. You may come in a day early, work the hospitality suite the first afternoon and the next 4 days do 8 hours in the booth, then a half day on the last day of the convention and arrive home on the 5th or 6th day. Of course you have to rest and in some situations you come home for 3 or 5 days but then you are on the next plane out of town on your way to another trade show. In between trade shows you are learning and rehearsing the pitch about an entirely different company.

I didn't do trade shows very long. It was hard to do trade shows, manufacture magic, work at restaurants, do kids birthday parties and school assemblies, and be a good Dad and husband at the same time. In the end I lost my marriage. Not what I wanted. I was too focused on being the best entertainer I could be. So one day I woke up with no wife, gave up doing trade shows, sold my magic equipment manufacturing, stopped working at restaurants, and decided to spend more time with my kids. I should have left my ego in the magic trunk. Later I limited myself to a few big shows and about 150 magic shows a year. In addition to my other entertainment activities I teach magic privately to a handful of students and spend more time with my family.

Trade shows are hard work and really pay well but are hard on the body. If you want to do trade shows, I advise you to do them when you are younger. As you get older it takes a toll on your body. Don't get me wrong, there are still some that have been doing tradeshows for 40 or more years. My hats are off to them, it must be real magic to do it that long.

Health Maintenance/ Insurance

As mentioned in other sections of this book health insurance may be a requirement for employment in certain situations. Nevertheless, as my mother, a nurse, has frequently reminded me, being an entertainer can be a very stressful and physically challenging occupation. Get a medical checkup, including teeth and mental health.

Health care can be very expensive; however the new federal Affordable Health Care Act provides new approaches for obtaining health care /insurance. This involves major changes especially for those in lower income brackets.

Chapter 11

TERMINOLOGY

Many locations have terms that are unique for their setting, such as restaurants, ships, country clubs, nightclubs, theaters, convention centers, trade shows, etc. Here are some common terms that are used for these venues.

Restaurant Terms

Back of the house: Kitchen may include food preparation, freezer, storage and dishwashing area.

Bartender: The person making drinks for the wait staff and guests.

Bar back: The person that gets the beer, wine, and whatever is needed when the bartender is busy.

BEHIND! Servers will announce they are behind with a tray of food and say "behind!" or "coming around!" to announce they are coming,

Busboy / Busgirl: A person that clears tables after the guests have left and may wipe the table and chairs.

Coming Around: Like "Behind!" When servers are coming from a blind corner or when you are facing another direction they will say "Coming Around". This is to let the entertainer know they are nearby usually with a tray or food.

Campers: Campers are people who are finished eating, paid their bill, and remain at their table.

Deuce or Double: A table that seats two people.

4 Top or 6 top: This term refers the number of people at a table.

Front of the House: The place where the host/hostess/maitre d' is located and also the dining room and the bar.

Host or Hostess: The person that you check in with to get seated. Give them your name and wait to be called.

Menu: A list of food and beverages for sale in the restaurant. It usually includes salads, entrees, desserts and drinks. It adds bonus points to your longevity as an entertainer at restaurants if you know the menu and can make recommendations (based on advice from management) to the guests.

Party: A group of people, "I'm going to entertain the party in the waiting area."

Server: This is a common name for the waiter or waitress.

Station: The area where servers get silverware, ice, food, condiments, glasses and water and may place your order and take care of your bill.

Slammed: It means very busy.

Stiffed: This term is used when a guest leaves no or very small tip.

Turning the Tables: Moving customers that are finished in order to make room for other guests. As an entertainer the wait staff will love you for having the knowledge to make it happen. The guests have ordered, eaten and paid their check and have asked to see the balloon guy or the magician. Never go and entertain when the check has been paid. I turn the table. I ask the guests to leave their seats and go to another area where I do a private show for them. Meanwhile the busboy and wait staff have reset the table and the host has seated new guests. You as an entertainer need to determine a diplomatic way to get people to leave the table after the bill has been paid.

Table Turn: Tables that had guests on them and are now reseated. Cruise ships and trains may schedule two seating times in order to accommodate all passengers.

86'd: When food is 86'd that means the restaurant is out of that item. When a person is 86'd they are no longer allowed in that establishment.

Ships, Yachts, and Boats

I live in San Diego which has many marinas. I have worked on several large 50' to 100' yachts. If you get a call to work a private yacht it is very important to know your way around the yacht.

We have harbor excursions that take guests out on the bay and one hotel has a turn of the century paddle wheeler. This is a Navy town and we have a large aircraft carrier that is a museum and a party location/ venue.

We also get bookings on smaller Navy ships as part of their family cruises. The ship will leave port for a few days with family, friends, navy personnel, and entertainers. Everyone gets a feel for what it's like to live on a naval vessel.

Some terms you need to know about vessels of all sizes:

Port and Starboard: Port is left and starboard is right.

Port and left are short words and so is red for the running light color. Right and starboard are longer words and so is green for the running light color. If you are standing on the bow (the front of the ship) looking ahead as the ship is underway (sailing/moving), the left running lights are red and the right running lights are green

Aboard: Being on the vessel

Aft: Toward the rear of the vessel.

Ahead: The ship is moving forward.

Batten down: Secure the loose materials and hatches.

Below: The space beneath the main deck.

Bow: The front of the vessel.

Bridge: Usually an elevated area where personnel control the vessel.

Bulkhead: The walls inside a ship.

Cabin: A living space for the passengers or crew.

Compartment: A larger area containing, bunks (beds), and/or lockers. The compartment on my ship slept 50 people.

Cleat: A piece of metal with projecting ends that is attached to the vessel and is used for connecting a rope (Line is the correct term) to it. The other end of the rope is fastened to another object such as a pier or another boat.

Fathom: A measurement of 6 feet of water or rope.

Forward: Toward the bow.

Galley: The kitchen.

Gunwale: The outside edges of the vessel.

Head: Restroom/toilet

Knot: A measurement of speed equal to one nautical mile per hour.

Line: Another name for rope.

Midship: The mid section of the vessel.

Passage way: The hallway of the vessel.

Mess: Eating area for the ship's crew.

Running lights: Lights displayed on the side of the vessel. Left side is red and right side is green.

Stern: The rear of the vessel
Underway: When the vessel is moving.

Now entertainer, you should be able to find your way around a ship, yacht, or boat. You won't be lost like I was as a boy playing on the old mothballed ships in the Philadelphia Naval Shipyard where my Dad was the Commanding Officer or on my first ship out of boot camp, the U.S.S. Constellation CVA-64.

Stage, Dinner Theater, Club

What about a theater, comedy club, dinner theater or magic club?

If you are hired for a dinner theater and you're going to be on stage, you might get an e-mail that reads like this: "Set the drums on the upper stage right, piano stage left and the microphone center stage." You want to learn some theater terms. Here's an easy way to remember stage right and stage left stuff, as explained by my father and mother who were in Community Theater when I was young.

Stage: Usually an elevated space visible to an audience...

Up Stage: The area of the stage that is the farthest from the audience.

Center Stage: The middle of the stage facing the audience.

Down Stage: The area of the stage that is the closest to the audience.

Stage Right: The right side of the stage facing the audience.

Stage Left: The left side of the stage from the performers view facing the audience.

Blocking: Where you should be on the stage during the performance. The time may vary when going from A to B on a new stage. A magician's assistant should practice blocking so that he/she knows when to come out and where to stand at any given time during the show.

Script: A written text with guidelines for the entertainers for a specific performance.

Convention Centers/Trade Shows

Convention centers are usually located in large cities. Some are larger than a football field. I have done many trade shows at large convention centers. Sometimes it takes 20 minutes to go from your booth to a restroom. Convention centers may be run by Unions. Many events such as graduations, sports, trade shows, etc. are held in convention centers. Maps are available showing the locations of exhibit halls, meeting rooms, and ballrooms.

It is advisable to arrive early at a convention center if you have never been there before in order to locate the significant areas you will be working. You can also go on line to get a footprint/layout of the convention center.

Trade Show Terms:

Air Walls: Large tall walls that are used to change the room size.

Aisle Signs: Signs usually suspended indicating aisle numbers and letters.

Booth Number: This is the number to identify your booth at the trade show.

Exhibit Booth: This is a specific constructed area with logos and colors to identify where the products are exhibited and the sales team is located.

Exhibit Directory: This is a book that will list where all the exhibit booths are located and may have some advertisements of local attractions and places to eat. It may also have a map of the exhibit hail and a map of the convention center or hotel as well as a map of the city.

Hospitality Suite: This is a room that your client will host. The client will invite his customers and dealers to the hospitality suite for food, drinks, and you may be entertaining in his booth at the trade show.

Pipe and Drape: If you needed a small dressing room or a back curtain you may request this. It's usually a pipe across the top of two stanchions holding a black drape to the floor. Sometimes the tradeshow booths are separated with pipe and drape as walls.

Riser: A small platform for the performer or product. (It's more comfortable to stand on than a cement floor)

Internet/Computer Terms

You absolutely need to know the terms used by internet and other technical devices. Purchase books, practice, and study. This book will not provide all of this information. It assumes that you know the meaning of common terms such as: internet, smart phone, laptop, notebook, desktop, Google, blog, Twitter, My Space, social networks, e-mail, texting, web site, internet service provider (ISP) etc.

Chapter 12

MISCELLANEOUS

Toilet Paper (TP)

Guess how many times I've made a stop at a gas station and guess what? NO TP. One night I was doing late Grad Nights for 2 schools and on the way to the school I stopped at a gas station and discovered there was no TP. No problem because I have a spare roll behind the seat of my car.

I'm coming home at 3 am and stop at another gas station and guess what? NO TP. but oh no, I left my TP at the first gas station. And did the attendant have any? "I don't know where they keep that stuff".

I had to go find another gas station. TP, Important stuff.

DON'T (The top 15 Don'ts)

1. Cut off any one while driving, it may be your client.

2. Flirt with the opposite sex while working.

3. Bite your nails on the way to the job.

4. Leave home later than planned. Don't be late

5. Eat spicy foods 6 hours before show time.

6. Drink alcohol on the day before or day of the event.

7. Wait until the day of the event to gas up your vehicle.

8. Enter your event smelling of cigarettes, cigars, marijuana, or alcohol.

9. Take unnecessary drugs including prescriptions Be aware Of potential dangers

10. Get into arguments with anyone before an event.

11. Use bad language or cuss at an event.

12. Tell dirty or "in bad taste" or "blue" jokes in mixed company.

13. Wear too much cologne or perfume.

14. Talk or text while driving.

15. Use your cell phone during show time unless you are on break.

Final Thoughts

The A, B, C's of being a professional entertainer are:
Always arrive early for the job.
Allow extra time for bad traffic and parking problems.
Always enjoy being an entertainer.
Always honor your "holds".
Be aware of your surroundings and know where the exits and restrooms are located.
Be better dressed than the guests attending the event.

Be helpful, be part of the team.
Be relaxed, not rushed.
Be clean, smell good.
Become skilled in keeping accurate records.
Be on time.
Carry lots of business cards and use appropriately.
Know whether the business card you pass out should be your agents or your own.
Call the client if you think you may be late.
Call the client a couple of days ahead to see if there are any changes.
Casual dress does not mean jeans with holes and flip flops.
Continue to grow in your skill – Practice, Practice, Practice.
Cough drops smell like alcohol, mints smell like mints.

Horror Stories

A while ago I was working for a major telecommunications company. They paid me really well to go to 8 of their distribution offices and introduce a new product for their sales staff. I went to each location and did a magic show at their luncheon and threaded their product message between the magic. All 7 locations were a great success.

The last show was to be in the penthouse at a well known hotel in San Francisco with the General Manager of the 7 other locations. The Chief Financial Officer (CFO) and the President of the company and other managers were there. I was briefed earlier not to use the CFO on stage as he is a bit shy.

I began doing some close-up magic before and during lunch. After lunch I would do a 15 minute presentation to show the
new product. In previous acts I would take watches, sort of a pick pocket kind of thing, and the watch could end up in a sealed envelope in someone's pocket, or in most cases I would say here's your watch and get a great round of applause. This was a crowd of about 50 people.

I started my walk-around and doing sleight-of-hand magic from table to table. I noticed one of the guests had a watch with a leather band. I proceeded to do my sponge ball routine and took his watch and put it into my jacket pocket. I finished the routine and did a few more tricks.

We were then asked to take our seats for lunch and I did a few more tricks at my table. After lunch I did my show to a great applause and went to the valet to pick up my car.

While waiting for my car I put my hand into the pocket and oops, I forgot to return the guest's watch. Yikes, this was a first for me.

I thought I could go back and as an encore produce the watch. When I went to the banquet room the doors were closed. The sign on a pedestal read "Meeting in session, do not disturb". I went in anyway and everyone looked at me, the gentleman at the podium said. . "Yes Mike? Can we help you?" It was the man whose watch I had in my hand and I said in a loud voice "I have your watch". The audience started to applaud and the gentleman said in a loud voice, "I'm sorry Magic Mike that is not my watch". Just as I was about to say "yes it is" his secretary ushered me into the hallway.

The audience was puzzled and still half applauding as the CFO continued his meeting. I was told by the secretary that the CFO had a phobia about people touching his stuff and he will never touch that watch again. They will probably donate it to a charity as it was a very expensive watch. I gave her the watch and never heard from that company again. I have never taken a watch since.

Another time I was doing a holiday party for a well known company in San Diego. I was doing the cocktail party from 6-7 PM in the foyer and the D.J. was setting up in the main room. I arrived 15 minutes before the event was to start and I went to introduce myself to the client. I started doing my strolling walk-around sleight of hand magic as people were arriving. The guests were standing and chatting with each other while trays of food and drinks were passed around as holiday music played.

I was about to start doing a trick when the D.J. asked me "Hey Magician, can you keep an eye on my stuff, I have to run back to my car!" I said "I'm working the room and not watching your stuff, but I will keep an eye out." About two minutes later when I was in the middle of a routine I heard "Where the blank, blank, are my, blank, CD's?" You could hear him on his cell phone cussing up a storm. And apparently whoever he was talking to must have told him they were on the kitchen table. He then went ballistic with cuss words. He had left his wireless microphone on and was cussing himself out all the way.

The audience lost interest in my entertaining and were listening to his every word. I went to the main dining room to unplug his system, but the client stopped me and told me the damage was done.

The D.J. walked into the foyer where I was performing and found the client. He told her he had to go home as he heard himself on the speakers. She said never mind, pack up your stuff, Your Fired! He walked past me and said was I live all the time I was gone, I said yes. He asked me why I didn't turn off his system and I told him that I tried but the client would not let me. It was too late, the damage had been done. So many people forget to turn their wireless microphones off when they are not using them.

Be very careful with wireless microphones. I saw a juggler one time do a great show on stage, but when he walked offstage, he had said some pretty mean things to his girlfriend and he was live for everyone to hear, because he forgot to turn off his microphone. When he went back to the stage the audience hated him.

On TV and live concerts you don't have to worry about turning off your microphone as the sound man takes care of that for you. But on the shows where you are running your own sound, be very careful with your wireless sound system.

Another time I heard one of our stage hands doing a microphone check, he too forgot to turn it off and he was hitting on one of the concession girls and the whole room could hear it, including him, as he quickly turned off the wireless headset.

Comics wear headsets as they walk back and forth on stage and as they are leaving the stage another comic is coming on and he too is wearing a head set. I've heard both of them talking at the same time. Sometimes, it's funny sometimes it's not.

I know a ventriloquist that has a lapel mike for his dummy, now that's funny.

Once I was working the foyer for a Bar Mitzvah, the D.J. was setting up a small sound and light system in the foyer and his main unit in the ballroom. I smelled something burning as he was setting up. I mentioned it to him and he told me to mind my own business since it's just the dust burning off of the light bulbs.

I followed the crowd into the ballroom to do some more magic when the fire alarm went off and the sound system in the foyer was on fire. It was put out before any of the guests got out of the room but it scarred everyone. As I was leaving I gave the D.J. the thumbs up sign. I never saw that D.J at another Mitzvah again.

At one time I went with a 15 piece orchestra on a boat for a harbor cruise. I asked the captain how much time we had before we sailed, he said "you can take all the time you need, this boat is not leaving until tomorrow, That one next to us leaves in 20 minutes". We were on the wrong boat. Did I mention it was pouring down rain? We made it just in the nick of time. Exhausted from the double set up, entertain for three hours then tear down and drive home. These are lessons to be learned.

Parking is so bad in certain parts of our city that I tell the client to leave a parking spot in front of their garage so I don't have to hoof it so far to get to their party.

One time I was doing a graduation party and came around the corner on the street that my party was on. I saw a sign across the garage door "Congratulations Graduate" and an empty parking space waiting for me. I walked into the home and the party was going strong. I started entertaining knowing the client will come up and introduce herself to me. After about 10 minutes the host of the party walked up and said, "Hi, who hired you?" I said Margie. She said "She lives 5 doors down and I believe they are having a graduation party as well". OOPS, I'm at the wrong house. She offered to call Margie and tell her that their magician was on the way.

One time a comic, a magician, and a band, was performing on the rooftop of a building for a grand opening celebration. There was just one problem. It was the day of the Blue Angels air show and this building was a couple of blocks from the Navy base. The audience could care less about the magic show, the comic, or the band. The planes were really loud but we still performed, did our job, and went home.

Remember that entertaining is your passion. You will appreciate the gigs when everything goes as planned and you may laugh when they don't.

As a fellow entertainer and as author of this book I look forward to sharing more of our experiences.

While working with Bernie Kaye's Entertainment Solutions, Mike Stilwell had associations with various entertainers. Here is a list of some acts that they presented over the years.

Accordionists	Dancers	Magicians
Acrobatic Acts	Dickens Carolers	Mimes
Astrologers	Dixieland Music	Mind Reader Acts
Bagpipers	Disc Jockeys	Money Booth
Balloon Decorators	Elves	Motivational Speakers
Balloon Sculptors	E. S. P. Shows	Murder Mystery Act
Banjo Players	Face Painters	One Man Bands
Barbershop Quartets	Flamenco Dancers	Palm Readers
Bavarian Music	Flamenco Guitarists	Pianists- Jazz
Bluegrass Musicians	Fortune Tellers	Pianists- Pop
Brass Ensembles	Game Shows	Pianists- Classical
Brazilian Music	Graphologists	Pianists (All Styles)
Brazilian Dancers	Greek Music	Polynesian Dancers
Cajun Music	Guitarists, Jazz &	Puppet Shows
Calypso Music	Rock	Reggae Music
Caribbean Music	Harpists	Renaissance Music
Caricaturists	Hawaiian Bands	Reptile Show
Carnival Games	Hawaiian Dancers	Rodeo Characters
Casino Theme Events	Herald Trumpeters	Santa Claus
Casino Games	Horse Race Video	Mrs. Claus
Celebrity	Human Statues	Square Dance Callers
Impersonators	Hypnotists	Steel Drum Bands
Celtic Musicians	Improvisation Comedy	Stilt Walkers
Chinese Lion Dancers	Instant Photos	String Trios &
Chinese Dragon	Irish Music	Quartets
Dancers	Israeli Music	Swing Dancers
Chinese Musicians	Italian Music	Table Heads
Classical Guitarists	Koto Music	Tarot Card Readers
Clowns	Jazz Bands	Theme Characters
Color Guards	Jugglers	Ventriloquists
Comedy Performers	Karaoke Disc Jockeys	Violinists
Computer Photos	Klezmer Music	Vocalists
Country Bands	Dance Teachers	
Cowboys , Cowgirls	Magic Shows	

INDEX

Made in the USA
Las Vegas, NV
17 August 2022

53439345R00074